Good Housekeeping

GREAT RECIPES FOR YOUR
BREAD MACHINE

Good Housekeeping

GREAT RECIPES FOR YOUR
BREAD MACHINE

100 tasty and innovative ideas

JOANNA FARROW

COLLINS & BROWN

First published in hardback in Great Britain in
2003 by Collins & Brown Limited
This paperback edition published in 2004.
The Chrysalis Building
Bramley Road
London W10 6SP

An imprint of **Chrysalis** Books Group

Published in association with
The National Magazine Company Limited.
Good Housekeeping is a registered trademark of
The National Magazine Company Limited.

13 5 7 9 8 6 4 2

British Library Cataloguing-in-Publication Data:
A catalogue record for this book is available
from the British Library.

ISBN 1-84340-223-8

Project Manager: Emma Baxter
Project editor: Janet Illsley
Designer: Christine Wood
Photography: Marie-Louise Avery
Food stylist: Joanna Farrow
Recipe tester: Charlotte Dunne

Reproduction by Tenon & Polert, Hong Kong
Printed and bound by Times Offset (M) Sdn.
Bhd, Malaysia
This book was typeset using Futura and Joanna

Breads pictured on jacket all photographed by
Mary Louise-Avery: **Front:** Pandolce p94;
Spine: Cranberry muffin cake p126;
Back, clockwise from top left: Basil and pine
nut stromboli p55, Farmhouse white loaf p14,
Focaccia p50, Pepper and pancetta buns p58.

NOTES

- Both metric and imperial measures are
  given for the recipes. Follow either set of
  measures, not a mixture of both, as they
  are not interchangeable.
- All spoon measures are level.
  1 tsp = 5ml spoon; 1 tbsp = 15ml spoon.
- Ovens must be preheated to the specified
  temperature.
- Large eggs should be used except where
  otherwise specified. Free-range eggs are
  recommended.
- The use of golden granulated, caster and
  icing sugar is recommended.

CONTENTS

FOREWORD

When I first had my bread maker at home, my children (aged 4, 7 and 9) were so excited to try it out. Even more so when they realised they could tuck into fresh hot bread within an hour on the fast setting. They'd always enjoyed making bread, particularly at weekends, and the kneading or dough throwing was the highlight. "Bash the dough rather than each other!" I'd say. Their bread was always light and airy because the punching and kneading went on a long time. But that activity had to be restricted to days when I had plenty of time to clear up.

The bread maker looked fab, shiny and chrome with a red light, and a timer that clearly indicated how many minutes they had to wait. We all used it more as a toy than an essential kitchen utensil. Then, rather like toys, the novelty wore off, and I decided that in my newly designed minimal kitchen there wasn't any room for it on the worksurface. I must confess that my bread machine has been lurking in the garage for a few months now.

Flicking through Joanna's inspiring recipes has made me want to rush to re-introduce the bread maker into my daily life. With innovative ideas such as Toasted seed and nut bread, and Chorizo and pine nut mini loaves, and classic combinations like Malted fruit loaf, Sticky gingerbread and even Carrot cake, who can blame me? Now I understand that you can use it as a tool to help so many types of recipes – it's not the limited machine the standard instruction booklet led me to believe. And there's no need to worry that your loaf might turn out like a brick. Because every recipe is triple tested to guarantee success, you can rest assured that your time, energy and expense will be rewarded.

Felicity Barnum-Bobb,
Cookery Editor

BREAD MACHINE BASICS

All bread machines knead, prove and bake excellent, fresh crusty bread, but models vary considerably. The main factors to take into account if you are buying a machine are the size of the loaf produced, and the bread making programmes available. Some cheaper models will make a good basic loaf, but one that is too small for a large family. The most versatile models give the option of different loaf sizes and lots of different programme settings, at a price. Bread machine loaves may not be cheaper than regular bought breads, but they do taste better. When you first acquire a bread machine, read the manual and use it to experiment with a basic loaf. This will help you to get to know your machine and give you the confidence to move on to more ambitious and interesting recipes.

PROGRAMMES

All bread machines offer a choice of programmes, some have a more comprehensive range than others. This book uses the settings that are available on most models, even basic ones. Most machines enable you to select the crust colour on certain programmes. Unless specified in a recipe, the crust selection is a matter of personal preference.

Some bread machines have a delayed timer setting so that you can pre-set the machine to bake bread that is fresh for breakfast, or ready when you return home from work. Don't use perishable ingredients like milk, eggs and cheese when you use this setting.

Basic or Normal is the most widely used programme, ideal for basic white bread and loaves that use mainly white flour with a small amount of brown or mixed grain flour. Some machines have a 'raisin beep' setting that indicates when you can add extra ingredients, like dried fruit, cheese and other items that you wouldn't want to be broken up during kneading. If your machine doesn't have this facility, add these ingredients towards the ends of the kneading cycle. (Most manuals provide a chart of the different cycle lengths so you can set a kitchen timer to remind you when to add them.)

Wholewheat or Wholemeal is used for breads with a high proportion of wholemeal or brown flour. This programme usually takes longer than the basic programme because brown flours take longer to rise. Some bread machines also have a multigrain programme, and again, multigrains take longer to rise.

Rapid or Quick is the accelerated programme that takes a much shorter time. The finished loaf won't be as well risen and therefore has a denser texture, but it is quite acceptable. Most of the 'simple breads' in this book can be made using this programme although it's best to avoid loaves with a high proportion of brown or wholemeal flour, or those with a low gluten content like rye and barley.

Dough mixes, kneads and proves the dough ready for shaping, second proving and baking in a conventional oven. Some machines have special programmes for different doughs, such as pizza bases, French bread and focaccia. Some also have a 'raisin setting' indicating when extra ingredients can be added to the dough. Don't worry if you're not around to take the dough out of the machine at the end of this programme, it will continue to prove but won't spoil.

Bake Only or Cake enables you to cook non-yeast teabreads and cakes – useful if you're already using the oven, or need to go out before the cake is baked. Deep Madeira-style cakes, fruitcakes and teabreads are most successful. Victoria sandwich cakes, whisked sponges and other cakes that need to go into a hot oven aren't suitable. Some machines mix and bake the cake; others bake only and use a timer, like a normal oven. The latter method is used in this book.

Before baking, remove the kneading blade and grease and line the bucket with baking parchment if the manual suggests you do so. Take care when testing to see if the cake is cooked, remember you're putting your hand inside a very hot oven!

BASIC INGREDIENTS

For most bread machines, there is a specific order in which you must add the ingredients to the bread bucket. Adding the ingredients in the wrong order can result in failure. Most machines require you to add the liquids first, followed by the dry ingredients and then the yeast, although some models use the reverse order. The order is especially important for machines that have a 'rest' period before the cycles start, as the yeast must be kept separate from the liquid, sugar and salt.

FLOURS

Strong white bread flour is the most effective bread maker flour and it is widely used in the book. White flour is ground from the wheat kernel once the outer bran is removed. 'Strong' flour is essential for bread machine baking as it has a higher proportion of protein, which promotes the formation of 'gluten'. This is the stretchy, elastic constituent of bread which, along with the yeast, gives bread its airy, stretchy texture. If possible use unbleached white flour which has not been chemically treated to whiten it.

Strong wholemeal bread flour is ground from the whole wheat kernel and has a coarser texture than white flour, with a fuller flavour and more nutrients. Because wholemeal flour contains wheat bran, the amount of gluten-forming proteins are reduced, resulting in a heavier, denser textured bread. For bread machine baking it's always best to use a proportion of strong white flour along with the wholemeal, to obtain a good texture.

Strong brown bread flour has a percentage of the bran removed and has a finer texture than wholemeal flour. Like wholemeal, it's best mixed with white flour in bread machine baking.

Granary and Malthouse flours contain a blend of white and wholemeal flour, mixed with malted wheat grains to give a slightly sweet, nutty flavour.

Rye flour makes a dark, close textured bread with plenty of flavour. Rye is most widely grown in northern and central Europe and features strongly in Scandinavian breads. Low in gluten, rye flour must be mixed with strong white flour in bread making. Rye flour that has a higher percentage of bran removed makes a lighter bread.

Spelt flour is derived from an ancient form of wheat and makes a tasty bread with a slightly nutty flavour. It is richer in nutrients than wheat flours and can sometimes be tolerated by people on wheat-free diets.

Cornmeal is ground from corn kernels and may have a fine or coarse texture. It is a good addition to breads but must be used in small quantities because of its low gluten content.

Barley flour has a mild, slightly sweet flavour and makes a soft textured bread. As it is very low in gluten, it must be mixed with strong white flour for bread machine baking.

Gluten-free flours are available from some large supermarkets, chemists and health food stores. Different forms are available, but they all contain a mixture of different starches and gluten-free flours, such as potato, rice, pea and soya flour. Some have added vegetable fibre, to produce a brown loaf. Only gluten-free flours that are specifically designed for bread making and bread machines are suitable. Ordinary gluten-free flours won't work.

YEAST

Only easy-blend dried yeast is suitable for use in bread machines and it is essential to measure the quantity precisely. If there is insufficient yeast the dough won't rise; too much yeast will cause the dough to deflate during baking. Don't use yeast that is passed its 'use by' date.

SALT

This is an essential ingredients in breads, even if you don't like a particularly salty flavour. Salt controls fermentation and strengthens gluten structure. When adding salt to the bucket, keep it away from the yeast as it will prevent activation; this is particularly important with machines that have a 'rest' period before mixing. Measure salt accurately.

SUGAR

Sugar helps to activate yeast, and lends a soft texture and good crust to breads. Unrefined brown sugars have more flavour than white sugars, and honey, treacle and maple syrup are good alternatives to vary the taste.

FATS

Most recipes in this book use a small quantity of butter to enrich the bread, add flavour and improve the keeping quality. Non-dairy margarines can be substituted for those on special diets. In some recipes olive oil is used instead.

LIQUIDS

Unless your machine states otherwise, liquids should be cold when they are added to the machine. Many of the recipes in this book use milk, which gives bread a slightly softer texture and improves its keeping quality. Don't use fresh milk on a time delay programme, use water instead and add a couple of tablespoons of milk powder to the bucket if you like.

HINTS FOR PERFECT BAKING

- If you are trying a new recipe, check the consistency of the dough after a few minutes of mixing. At this stage you can add a little more flour if the dough is sticky and wet, or a little more water if it's dry and crumbly.
- Keep a plastic spatula handy for pushing down any pieces of dry dough or flour that stick to the sides of the bucket during the early stages of mixing and kneading.
- Don't be tempted to add more than the recommended quantities of additional flavourings or the texture of the bread may be spoilt.
- Avoid lifting the lid once the proving and baking cycles start or you'll risk a sunken loaf.
- Not all loaves will have a domed surface after baking. Highly enriched breads and those that contain a high proportion of brown or rye flour are more likely to have a flat surface or slightly sunken one. This won't affect the flavour or quality of the bread.
- Unless your bread maker has a 'keep warm' setting after baking (usually about an hour), the loaf is best removed from the machine as soon as possible once baking is complete. Otherwise condensation that occurs as the machine cools may turn the bread soggy.
- If the kneading blade gets stuck inside the loaf after baking, carefully ease it out as soon as the bread is cool enough to handle.
- If you find it difficult to remove the kneading blade from the bucket after taking out the bread, half fill the bucket with warm water and leave to soak for about 10 minutes before easing the blade away.
- Conventional bread recipes cannot be converted easily for use in a bread machine as they use a different ratio of yeast, flour and liquid. However, as you gain experience, you'll become adept at experimenting with the recipes in this book to try different flavour combinations.
- Some bread machines have a specific programme for making breads using bread mixes. If you want to try these, refer to your manual to see if they are suitable for your machine.

1

SIMPLE BREADS

FARMHOUSE WHITE LOAF

LIGHTENED WHOLEMEAL BREAD

MOLASSES BROWN BREAD

MALTED GRAIN LOAF

MIXED GRAIN LOAF

SOFT GRAIN OATMEAL BREAD

BARLEY BREAD

TOASTED SEED AND NUT BREAD

RYE AND CARAWAY BREAD

CHALLAH

WHEAT BERRY BREAD

CHUNKY WALNUT BREAD

SWEET POLENTA LOAF

FRUITED MUESLI LOAF

ORANGE AND ALMOND BREAD

Farmhouse white loaf

MAKES 1 LARGE LOAF: ABOUT 12 SLICES

PER SLICE: 180 cals; 3g fat; 34g carbohydrate

1 tsp easy-blend dried yeast

500g (1lb 2oz) strong white bread flour, plus extra to sprinkle

1 tbsp caster sugar

2 tbsp milk powder

1½ tsp salt

25g (1oz) butter

350ml (12fl oz) water

This is the simplest bread of all, a great starting point for the new bread machine baker. Light, open textured, and with a traditional home baked crust, it's a staple recipe that can be relied on time and time again. *Illustrated*

1 Put the ingredients into the bread maker bucket, following the order and method specified in the manual.

2 Fit the bucket into the bread maker and set to the basic programme with a crust of your choice. Press start.

3 Just before baking starts, brush the top of the dough with water and sprinkle with flour. If preferred, slash the top of the bread lengthways with a sharp knife, taking care not to scratch the bucket.

4 After baking, remove the bread from the machine and shake out on to a wire rack to cool.

Lightened wholemeal bread

MAKES 1 LARGE LOAF: ABOUT 12 SLICES

PER SLICE: 150 cals; 3g fat; 29g carbohydrate

1½ tsp easy-blend dried yeast

400g (14oz) strong wholemeal flour

100g (3½oz) strong white bread flour

1½ tsp salt

1 tbsp dark muscovado sugar

25g (1oz) butter

350ml (12fl oz) water

Machine baked breads made entirely with wholemeal flour tend to have a heavy texture because their high bran content reduces the efficiency of gluten and inhibits rising. Adding a proportion of white flour lightens the dough without compromising the traditional brown bread flavour. Alternatively you could use all brown flour, which has some of the bran removed.

1 Put the ingredients into the bread maker bucket, following the order and method specified in the manual.

2 Fit the bucket into the bread maker and set to the programme recommended in the manual, usually wholewheat. Select the crust of your choice and press start.

3 After baking, remove the bread from the machine and shake out on to a wire rack to cool.

Molasses brown bread

MAKES 1 LARGE LOAF: ABOUT 12 SLICES

PER SLICE: 170 cals; 2g fat; 33g carbohydrate

1 tsp easy-blend dried yeast
200g (7oz) strong white bread flour
250g (9oz) strong brown bread flour
50g (2oz) buckwheat flour
2 tsp ground allspice
1½ tsp salt
3 tbsp molasses or black treacle
25g (1oz) butter
350ml (12fl oz) water

A deliciously moist, dark and sweet loaf that's great for serving with hot, steaming casseroles or wintry bean dishes so you can mop up the thick, flavourful juices. The spice adds a mild warmth to the bread, but can be left out for a less pronounced flavour.

1 Put the ingredients into the bread maker bucket, following the order and method specified in the manual.
2 Fit the bucket into the bread maker and set to the basic programme with a crust of your choice. Press start.
3 After baking, remove the bread from the machine and shake out on to a wire rack to cool.

Malted grain loaf

MAKES 1 LARGE LOAF: ABOUT 12 SLICES

PER SLICE: 190 cals; 4g fat; 32g carbohydrate

1 tsp easy-blend dried yeast
500g (1lb 2oz) Granary or malthouse flour
1½ tsp salt
2 tbsp milk powder
2 tbsp malt extract
25g (1oz) butter
350ml (12fl oz) water
2 tbsp sunflower seeds to sprinkle

Mixed grain flour makes a moist, light loaf with plenty of texture and natural sweetness. Use Granary or Malthouse flour, which both contain a blend of wholemeal, white and rye flour with additional malted grains. A simple, versatile, everyday bread.

1 Put the ingredients into the bread maker bucket, following the order and method specified in the manual.
2 Fit the bucket into the bread maker and set to the programme recommended in the manual, usually multigrain. Press start.
3 Just before baking starts, brush the top of the dough with water and sprinkle with the sunflower seeds. Slash the top of the dough lengthways with a sharp knife, taking care not to scratch the bucket.
4 After baking, remove the bread from the machine and shake out on to a wire rack to cool.

Mixed grain loaf

MAKES 1 LARGE LOAF: ABOUT 12 SLICES

PER SLICE: 180 cals; 4g fat; 33g carbohydrate

1 tsp easy-blend dried yeast

300g (11oz) strong white bread flour

100g (3½oz) strong wholemeal bread flour

50g (2oz) bulgur wheat

25g (1oz) millet grain

2 tbsp linseed

2 tbsp porridge oats or wheat flakes, plus extra to sprinkle

1½ tsp salt

1 tbsp golden caster sugar

25g (1oz) butter

350ml (12fl oz) water

Unlike the previous recipe, this rustic bread uses a 'homemade' blend of cereals and seeds, illustrating the bread machine's versatility. The bulgur wheat and millet are not pre-cooked before they are added to the bread maker, resulting in an interesting variety of textures. Don't be tempted to add too many grains though, as the dough simply wouldn't rise!

1 Put the ingredients into the bread maker bucket, following the order and method specified in the manual.

2 Fit the bucket into the bread maker and set to the programme recommended in the manual, usually multigrain, with the crust of your choice. Press start.

3 Just before baking starts, brush the top of the dough with water and sprinkle with the extra oats or wheat flakes.

4 After baking, remove the bread from the machine and shake out on to a wire rack to cool.

Soft grain oatmeal bread

MAKES 1 LARGE LOAF: ABOUT 12 SLICES

PER SLICE: 170 cals; 3g fat; 33g carbohydrate

1¼ tsp easy-blend dried yeast

300g (11oz) strong white bread flour

100g (3½oz) medium oatmeal, plus extra to sprinkle

75g (3oz) strong wholemeal or brown bread flour

1 tsp salt

3 tbsp clear or thick honey

150ml (¼ pint) natural yogurt

25g (1oz) butter

200ml (7fl oz) water

The combination of oatmeal and yogurt gives this loaf a lovely moist texture that is close without being heavy. Honey provides a sweet, almost fruity flavour, making it ideal bread for toasting. *Illustrated*

1 Put the ingredients into the bread maker bucket, following the order and method specified in the manual.
2 Fit the bucket into the bread maker and set to the basic programme with a light crust. Press start.
3 Just before baking, brush the top of the dough with water and sprinkle with oatmeal.
4 After baking, remove the bread from the machine and shake out on to a wire rack to cool.

Barley bread

MAKES 1 LARGE LOAF: ABOUT 12 SLICES

PER SLICE: 180 cals; 3g fat; 33g carbohydrate

1 large egg

200ml (7fl oz) milk

1 tsp easy-blend dried yeast

375g (13oz) strong white bread flour

125g (4oz) barley flour

1 tsp salt

2 tbsp sunflower honey

25g (1oz) butter

Barley lends bread a sweet nutty flavour and a firm, cakey texture, but because of it's low gluten content, it must be mixed with strong flour to give the dough sufficient lift.

1 Lightly beat the egg in a measuring jug. Add the milk, then make up to 350ml (12fl oz) with water.
2 Put the ingredients into the bread maker bucket, following the order and method specified in the manual.
3 Fit the bucket into the bread maker and set to the basic programme with a crust of your choice. Press start.
4 Just before baking starts, make shallow diagonal cuts across the bread then repeat in the other direction to create a diamond pattern. Take care not to scratch the bucket.
5 After baking, remove the bread from the machine and shake out on to a wire rack to cool.

Toasted seed and nut bread

MAKES 1 MEDIUM LOAF: ABOUT 10 SLICES

PER SLICE: 240 cals; 12g fat; 32g carbohydrate

75g (3oz) unblanched hazelnuts, finely chopped

2 tbsp each of poppy, sesame, sunflower and pumpkin
seeds

1 tsp easy-blend dried yeast

375g (13oz) strong white bread flour

25g (1oz) wheat bran

1 tsp salt

2 tsp light muscovado sugar

2 tbsp hazelnut or sunflower oil

300ml (½ pint) water, plus 1 tbsp

This earthy, rustic bread has all the intense flavour and bite of breads that you buy from the best deli's and bakers. Seeds provide vital nutrients, making this a good breakfast bread, or one to serve with snacks and salads. *Illustrated*

1 Toast the hazelnuts in a dry frying pan over a gentle heat, stirring, until they begin to colour, about 2 minutes. Add the seeds and fry gently for a further 1 minute. Take off the heat.

2 Put all the remaining ingredients in the bread maker bucket, following the order and method specified in the manual. Set aside 2 tbsp of the toasted nut mixture; add the rest to the bucket.

3 Fit the bucket into the bread maker and set to the basic programme with a crust of your choice. Press start.

4 Just before baking starts, brush the top of the dough with water and sprinkle with the reserved nuts and seeds.

5 After baking, remove the bread from the machine and shake out on to a wire rack to cool.

Rye and caraway bread

MAKES 1 MEDIUM LOAF: ABOUT 10 SLICES

PER SLICE: 180 cals; 3g fat; 37g carbohydrate

1½ tsp easy-blend dried yeast

300g (11oz) strong white bread flour

150g (5oz) stoneground rye flour

1 tbsp caraway seeds, plus extra to sprinkle

1½ tsp salt

15g (½oz) butter

2 tbsp black treacle

1 tbsp milk powder

300ml (½ pint) water

Rye flour creates a tangy flavour and dense texture that's familiar in Northern European breads. Because rye is low in gluten, it is best combined with strong white flour to make a decent loaf, with a characteristic craggy top. Don't expect it to rise as much as other machine-made breads.

1 Put the ingredients into the bread maker bucket, following the order and method specified in the manual.

2 Fit the bucket into the bread maker and set to the basic programme with a crust of your choice. Press start.

3 Just before baking starts, brush the top of the dough with water and sprinkle with extra caraway seeds.

4 After baking, remove the bread from the machine and shake out on to a wire rack to cool.

Challah

MAKES 1 MEDIUM LOAF: ABOUT 10 SLICES

PER SLICE: 200 cals; 6g fat; 34g carbohydrate

2 medium eggs, plus 1 egg yolk

About 100ml (3½fl oz) water

1 tsp easy-blend dried yeast

400g (14oz) strong white bread flour

1 tsp salt

3 tbsp thin honey

40g (1½oz) butter

Poppy seeds to sprinkle

A Jewish Sabbath bread, Challah is traditionally baked as a coiled or plaited loaf, liberally sprinkled with poppy seeds. This bread machine version may look very different, but it is similarly based on a dough enriched with egg, honey and butter, and has a comparable flavour.

1 Lightly beat the eggs and egg yolk in a measuring jug. Make up to 275ml (9fl oz) with water.

2 Put the ingredients into the bread maker bucket, following the order and method specified in the manual.

3 Fit the bucket into the bread maker and set to the basic programme with a medium crust. Press start.

4 Just before baking starts, brush the top of the dough with water and sprinkle with poppy seeds. Make several shallow cuts widthways across the bread, taking care not to scratch the bucket.

5 After baking, remove the bread from the machine and shake out on to a wire rack to cool.

Wheat berry bread

MAKES 1 LARGE LOAF: ABOUT 12 SLICES

PER SLICE: 180 cals; 3g fat; 36g carbohydrate

75g (3oz) wheat berries

1 tsp easy-blend dried yeast

300g (11oz) strong white or soft grain bread flour

200g (7oz) strong wholemeal bread flour

1½ tsp salt

1 tbsp golden caster sugar

25g (1oz) butter

350ml (12fl oz) water

Wheat flakes to sprinkle

Whole wheat berries give this rustic loaf plenty of texture and flavour. As the berries (or whole wheat grains) have only their outer coating removed, they must be pre-cooked to soften them before adding to bread mixtures. Using a mixture of white and wholemeal flour works well here.

1 Cook the wheat berries in plenty of boiling water for 20 minutes or until softened. Drain.

2 Put the ingredients into the bread maker bucket, following the order and method specified in the manual, adding the berries with the water.

3 Fit the bucket into the bread maker and set to the basic programme with a crust of your choice. Press start.

4 Just before baking starts, brush the top of the dough with water and sprinkle with the wheat flakes.

5 After baking, remove the bread from the machine and shake out on to a wire rack to cool.

Chunky walnut bread

MAKES 1 LARGE LOAF: ABOUT 12 SLICES
PER SLICE: 200 cals; 8g fat; 28g carbohydrate

100g (3½oz) walnut pieces
1 tsp easy-blend dried yeast
350g (12oz) strong wholemeal bread flour
150g (5oz) strong white bread flour
2 tbsp light muscovado sugar
3 tbsp walnut oil
1½ tsp salt
350ml (12fl oz) water

Lightly toasted chopped walnuts and wholemeal flour make a full flavoured bread that's great at any time of day, whether you spread it with jam or marmalade, use it for sandwiches, or to mop up the juices from a wintry casserole. If you haven't any walnut oil, use sunflower oil instead.

1 Toast the walnuts in a dry frying pan over a gentle heat for 2–3 minutes until coloured. Take off the heat.
2 Put the remaining ingredients into the bread maker bucket, following the order and method specified in the manual. Add the walnuts.
3 Fit the bucket into the bread maker and set to the basic programme with a crust of your choice. Press start.
4 Just before baking starts, score the dough diagonally with a sharp knife, taking care not to scratch the bucket.
5 After baking, remove the bread from the machine and shake out on to a wire rack to cool.

Sweet polenta loaf

MAKES 1 LARGE LOAF: ABOUT 12 SLICES
PER SLICE: 180 cals; 2g fat; 36g carbohydrate

1 tsp easy-blend dried yeast
375g (13oz) strong white bread flour
125g (4oz) polenta, plus extra to sprinkle
1 tsp salt
3 tbsp golden caster sugar
25g (1oz) butter
100ml (3½fl oz) milk
200ml (7fl oz) water

Polenta gives this bread a subtle, golden colour and light, almost cakey texture – great for topping with homemade strawberry jam and cream, or simply toasting for breakfast. For a lunch or picnic bread, omit the sugar and use 2 tablespoons of olive oil instead of the butter. This bread can also be made using cornmeal (sometimes called maizemeal). It's more finely ground than polenta but produces a loaf with a similar flavour.

1 Put the ingredients into the bread maker bucket, following the order and method specified in the manual.
2 Fit the bucket into the bread maker and set to the basic programme with a crust of your choice. Press start.
3 Just before baking starts, brush the top of the dough with water and sprinkle lightly with polenta.
4 After baking, remove the bread from the machine and shake out on to a wire rack to cool.

Fruited muesli loaf

MAKES 1 MEDIUM LOAF: ABOUT 10 SLICES

PER SLICE: 200 cals; 3g fat; 39g carbohydrate

1½ tsp easy-blend dried yeast

225g (8oz) strong white bread flour

100g (3½oz) strong brown bread flour

100g (3½oz) natural muesli

1 tsp salt

1 tbsp clear honey

50g (2oz) raisins

25g (1oz) butter

250ml (8fl oz) water

2 tbsp clear honey to glaze

Plenty of dried fruit and muesli make this wholesome loaf the natural choice for breakfast, either freshly baked or lightly toasted. Make sure you use muesli that's free from added sugar and salt. *Illustrated*

1 Put the ingredients into the bread maker bucket, following the order and method specified in the manual.

2 Fit the bucket into the bread maker and set to the programme recommended in the manual, usually multigrain. Select the crust of your choice and press start.

3 After baking, remove the bread from the machine and shake out on to a wire rack to cool. Brush the top of the loaf with honey to glaze.

Orange and almond bread

MAKES 1 LARGE LOAF: ABOUT 12 SLICES

PER SLICE: 230 cals; 7g fat; 38g carbohydrate

100g (3½oz) flaked almonds

1 tsp easy-blend dried yeast

500g (1lb 2oz) strong white bread flour

2 tsp ground cinnamon

1 tsp salt

3 tbsp light muscovado sugar

2 tbsp sweet almond oil or sunflower oil

Finely grated zest of 2 oranges

250ml (8fl oz) freshly squeezed orange juice, mixed with 100ml (3½fl oz) water

Icing sugar to dust

Subtly sweetened and mildly flavoured, this light textured bread is good for toast and marmalade, or later in the day with jam or other preserves.

1 Lightly crumble the flaked almonds into a frying pan and toast over a low heat for about 2 minutes until lightly coloured. Take off the heat.

2 Put the remaining ingredients into the bread maker bucket, following the order and method specified in the manual. Reserve 2 tbsp of the toasted almonds; add the rest to the bucket. Set to the basic programme with a crust of your choice and press start.

3 Just before baking starts, brush the top of the dough with water and sprinkle with the reserved almonds.

4 After baking, remove the bread from the machine and shake out on to a wire rack to cool. Dust lightly with icing sugar to serve.

2

SAVOURY ENRICHED BREADS

FENNEL, GREEN PEPPERCORN AND GRUYÈRE BREAD

HERBY SUN-DRIED TOMATO AND PARMESAN BREAD

ITALIAN ROSEMARY AND RAISIN LOAF

MIXED OLIVE BREAD

SPICED PARSNIP AND CORIANDER LOAF

CAERPHILLY, SAGE AND APPLE BREAD

GRAINY MUSTARD AND BEER BREAD

DILL AND POTATO BREAD

CHICKPEA, CHILLI AND ONION LOAF

SEEDED HORSERADISH AND HERB BREAD

SPICED SEEDED BREAD WITH MANGO

BEETROOT AND CARAWAY LOAF

BASIL, MANCHEGO AND SERRANO BREAD

MUSHROOM AND GARLIC BREAD

Fennel, green peppercorn and Gruyère bread

MAKES 1 MEDIUM LOAF: ABOUT 10 SLICES

PER SLICE: 180 cals; 4g fat; 31g carbohydrate

25g (1oz) butter

200g (7oz) fennel bulb, finely chopped

2 tbsp green peppercorns in brine, drained

1 tsp easy-blend dried yeast

400g (14oz) strong white bread flour

1 tsp salt

275ml (9fl oz) water

2 tbsp chopped fresh fennel

50g (2oz) Gruyère cheese, grated

This is one of those flavoured breads that you'd find difficult to buy. It's a perfect partner for fish stews and soups, or a special cheeseboard. Sautéed Florence fennel is enveloped in a light dough, along with Gruyère, green peppercorns and herbs. *Illustrated*

1 Melt the butter in a frying pan, add the chopped fennel bulb and fry gently for 5 minutes until very soft. Lightly crush the peppercorns using a pestle and mortar, or a small bowl and the end of a rolling pin.

2 Put the yeast, flour, salt and water into the bread maker bucket, following the order and method specified in the manual. Add the fennel herb and crushed peppercorns.

3 Fit the bucket into the bread maker and set to the basic programme with raisin setting, if applicable. Select the crust of your choice and press start. Add the sautéed fennel and cheese to the bucket when the machine beeps, or halfway through the kneading cycle.

4 After baking, remove the bread from the machine and shake out on to a wire rack to cool.

Herby sun-dried tomato and Parmesan bread

MAKES 1 MEDIUM LOAF: ABOUT 10 SLICES

PER SLICE: 180 cals; 3g fat; 33g carbohydrate

40g (1½oz) sun-dried tomatoes in oil, drained

3 tbsp sun-dried tomato paste

325ml (11fl oz) water

1½ tsp easy-blend dried yeast

425g (15oz) strong white bread flour

1 tsp salt

40g (1½oz) Parmesan cheese, freshly grated

2 tbsp finely chopped fresh oregano or rosemary

This is an excellent bread to serve warm with cold meats and cheeses, and for sandwiches. Sun-dried tomatoes and tomato paste impart a lively tang and interesting colour.

1 Finely chop the sun-dried tomatoes and mix with the tomato paste and water. Put the ingredients into the bread maker bucket, following the order and method specified in the manual, adding the cheese and herb after the flour.

2 Fit the bucket into the machine and set to the basic programme with a crust of your choice. Press start.

3 After baking, remove the bread from the machine and shake out on to a wire rack to cool.

Italian rosemary and raisin loaf

MAKES 1 MEDIUM LOAF: ABOUT 10 SLICES

PER SLICE: 240 cals; 7g fat; 40g carbohydrate

2 medium eggs

About 175ml (6fl oz) water

1 tsp easy-blend dried yeast

400g (14oz) strong white bread flour

1 tsp salt

3 tbsp chopped fresh rosemary

1 tbsp golden caster sugar

4 tbsp extra-virgin olive oil

125g (4oz) raisins

Small rosemary sprigs to finish

Enriched with eggs and olive oil, and dotted with raisins and rosemary, this loaf is based on an ancient Tuscan recipe. It's particularly good with soft, creamy cheeses. *Illustrated*

1 Lightly beat the eggs in a measuring jug. Make up the volume to 275ml (9fl oz) with water.

2 Put all the ingredients except the raisins into the bread maker bucket, following the order and method specified in the manual, adding the chopped rosemary after the flour.

3 Fit the bucket into the bread maker and set to the basic programme with raisin setting, if applicable. Select the crust of your choice and press start. Add the raisins when the machine beeps, or halfway through the kneading cycle.

4 Just before baking, press plenty of small rosemary sprigs into the surface of the dough.

5 After baking, remove the bread from the machine and shake out on to a wire rack to cool.

Mixed olive bread

MAKES 1 LARGE LOAF: ABOUT 12 SLICES

PER SLICE: 190 cals; 5g fat; 33g carbohydrate

1 tsp easy-blend dried yeast

500g (1lb 2oz) strong white bread flour

1½ tsp salt

1 tbsp caster sugar

3 tbsp extra-virgin olive oil

350ml (12fl oz) water

150g (5oz) pitted olives, roughly chopped

This easy bread is perfect for doorstep sandwiches, or for serving warm with soups or antipasto. Use the best pitted olives you can buy, mixing green and black ones if you like. For extra flavour, use olives marinated in spices and herbs, but don't be tempted to tip in the oil as well.

1 Put all the ingredients except the olives into the bread maker bucket, following the order and method specified in the manual.

2 Fit the bucket into the bread maker and set to the basic programme with raisin setting, if applicable. Select the crust of your choice and press start.

3 Reserve a tablespoonful of olives. Add the rest to the bucket when the machine beeps, or halfway through the kneading programme.

4 Just before baking, brush the surface of the dough with water and gently press in the reserved olives.

5 After baking, remove the bread from the machine and shake out on to a wire rack to cool.

Spiced parsnip and coriander loaf

MAKES 1 MEDIUM LOAF: ABOUT 10 SLICES

PER SLICE: 160 cals; 2g fat; 33g carbohydrate

150g (5oz) small parsnips, cut into small chunks

1 tsp easy-blend dried yeast

400g (14oz) strong white bread flour

1 tsp salt

1 tsp dried chilli flakes

½ tsp ground turmeric

1 tsp golden caster sugar

15g (½oz) butter

25g (1oz) chopped fresh coriander leaves

Use young tender parsnips, which mash well and give this bread a subtle, sweet flavour. If you prefer, use a finely chopped fresh chilli instead of dried chilli flakes. After baking, the loaf might sink slightly, but this won't adversely affect the texture or flavour.

1 Put the parsnips in a small pan, cover with water and bring to the boil. Cover and simmer for 10 minutes or until tender. Drain, reserving the cooking juices and mash well. Leave to cool. Measure 275ml (9fl oz) of the cooking liquid, making up to this quantity with water if necessary.

2 Put the ingredients into the bread maker bucket, following the order and method specified in the manual, adding the mashed parsnips, chilli and turmeric after the flour.

3 Fit the bucket into the bread maker and set to the basic programme with raisin setting, if applicable. Select a medium or dark crust and press start. Add the coriander when the machine beeps or towards the end of the kneading programme.

4 After baking, remove the bread from the machine and shake out on to a wire rack to cool.

Caerphilly, sage and apple bread

MAKES 1 MEDIUM LOAF: ABOUT 10 SLICES

PER SLICE: 210 cals; 4g fat; 38g carbohydrate

75g (3oz) dried apple, diced

150ml (¼ pint) boiling water

1 tsp easy-blend dried yeast

450g (1lb) strong softgrain bread flour

1 tsp salt

1 tbsp golden caster sugar

15g (½oz) butter

75g (3oz) Caerphilly or Cheshire cheese, crumbled into chunks

20 large fresh sage leaves, shredded, plus extra to scatter

This country-style bread is good eaten on its own, or with a chunk of cheese and an apple for a light lunch. It's a good recipe to experiment with, using different cheeses, dried fruit and herbs.

1 Soak the dried apple in the boiling water for 20 minutes. Drain well, reserving the liquid; make up to 275ml (9fl oz) with cold water.

2 Put all the ingredients except the apple, cheese and sage into the bread maker bucket, following the order and method specified in the manual.

3 Fit the bucket into the bread maker and set to the basic programme with raisin setting, if applicable. Select the crust of your choice and press start. Add the apple, cheese and sage when the machine beeps, or halfway through the kneading cycle.

4 Just before baking starts, lightly brush the top of the dough with water and scatter with extra sage leaves.

5 After baking, remove the bread from the machine and shake out on to a wire rack to cool.

Grainy mustard and beer bread

MAKES 1 MEDIUM LOAF: ABOUT 10 SLICES
PER SLICE: 200 cals; 3g fat; 37g carbohydrate

1 tsp easy-blend dried yeast

300g (11oz) strong white bread flour, plus extra to dust

200g (7oz) strong wholemeal bread flour

1 tsp salt

1 tbsp black treacle

3 tbsp strong grainy mustard

1 tsp Dijon mustard

25g (1oz) butter

300ml (½ pint) strong beer

Substituting beer, cider or fruit juice for the more familiar liquids in breads creates an interesting variety of flavours and textures. A rich, dark ale is the choice for this rustic lunch bread. Measure the beer and let it stand in the measuring jug for at least 30 minutes before use, to allow it to go flat and prevent it frothing out of the bread bucket.

1 Put the ingredients into the bread maker bucket, following the order and method specified in the manual, adding the mustards with the flour.

2 Fit the bucket into the bread maker and set to the basic programme. Select the crust of your choice and press start.

3 Just before baking, lightly brush the dough with water and sprinkle with a little extra flour. Using a sharp knife dipped in flour, make diagonal cuts across the surface, taking care not to scratch the bucket.

4 After baking, remove the bread from the machine and shake out on to a wire rack to cool.

Dill and potato bread

MAKES 1 SMALL LOAF: ABOUT 10 SLICES
PER SLICE: 160 cals; 1g fat; 35g carbohydrate

175g (6oz) potatoes, peeled and cut into small chunks

1 tsp easy-blend dried yeast

350g (12oz) strong white bread flour

50g (2oz) rye flour

1 tsp salt

1 tsp golden caster sugar

1 tbsp dill seeds, plus extra to sprinkle

2 tbsp skimmed milk powder

Milk to brush

This wonderful moist, dense textured bread is perfect with cold roast beef, ham and smoked fish. If you can't get dill seeds, try caraway instead.

1 Put the potatoes in a small pan, just cover with water and bring to the boil. Reduce the heat and simmer for 15 minutes until the potatoes are tender. Drain, reserving the liquid; measure 175ml (6fl oz), making up to this quantity with cold water if necessary. Leave to cool.

2 Put the ingredients into the bread maker bucket, following the order and method specified in the manual, adding the mashed potato and dill seeds with the flour.

3 Fit the bucket into the bread maker and set to the basic programme. Select the crust of your choice and press start. Check the dough once kneading has started, adding an extra 1–2 tbsp water if it is too dry.

4 Just before baking, brush the surface of the dough with milk and scatter with extra dill seeds.

5 After baking, remove the bread from the machine and shake out on to a wire rack to cool.

Chickpea, chilli and onion loaf

MAKES 1 MEDIUM LOAF: ABOUT 10 SLICES

PER SLICE: 190 cals; 5g fat; 34g carbohydrate

1 tsp easy-blend dried yeast

400g (14oz) strong white bread flour

1 tsp salt

3 tbsp olive oil

2 tsp golden caster sugar

1 small red onion, finely chopped

1 green chilli, deseeded and chopped

2 tsp cumin seeds, lightly crushed

200ml (7fl oz) water

100g (3½oz) canned chickpeas, rinsed and drained

Chickpea or gram flour is often used for bread making, but this recipe combines whole chickpeas with red onion, chilli and cumin, for an intensely savoury, spicy bread with an interesting, moist texture. Don't be tempted to add the remaining chickpeas from the can; keep them for a salad or vegetable dish. *Illustrated*

1 Put all the ingredients except the chickpeas into the bread maker bucket, following the order and method specified in the manual, adding the onion, chilli and cumin after the flour.

2 Fit the bucket into the bread maker and set to the basic programme with raisin setting, if applicable. Select the crust of your choice and press start. Add the chickpeas when the machine beeps, or halfway through the kneading cycle.

3 After baking, remove the bread from the machine and shake out on to a wire rack to cool.

Seeded horseradish and herb bread

MAKES 1 LARGE LOAF: ABOUT 12 SLICES

PER SLICE: 160 cals; 3g fat; 33g carbohydrate

1 tsp easy-blend dried yeast

450g (1lb) strong soft grain bread flour

50g (2oz) stoneground rye flour

1½ tsp salt

1 tbsp light muscovado sugar

1 tbsp dill seeds

2 tbsp chopped fresh parsley

2 tbsp grated hot horseradish, fresh or from a jar

25g (1oz) butter

350ml (12fl oz) water

Aromatic flavourings, such as horseradish and spices, make excellent additions to machine-made breads, because you only need a little to impart a distinctive flavour, so the texture of the dough is kept light. If you're lucky enough to get a fresh horseradish root, finely grate it and use in the same way as grated horseradish from a jar. With its slightly Swedish flavour, this bread is good with cheese, smoked fish and meats.

1 Put the ingredients into the bread maker bucket, following the order and method specified in the manual and adding the dill seeds, parsley and horseradish after the flour.

2 Fit the bucket into the bread maker and set to the basic programme with a crust of your choice. Press start.

3 After baking, remove the bread from the machine and shake out on to a wire rack to cool.

Spiced seeded bread with mango

MAKES 1 MEDIUM LOAF: ABOUT 10 SLICES

PER SLICE: 170 cals; 4g fat; 34g carbohydrate

12 cardamom pods

1 tbsp cumin seeds

1 tbsp coriander seeds

1 tbsp black onion seeds, plus extra to sprinkle

½ tsp dried chilli flakes

1 tsp ground turmeric

15g (½oz) fresh root ginger, finely chopped

½ tsp easy-blend dried yeast

400g (14oz) strong white bread flour

1 tsp salt

1 tsp golden caster sugar

2 tbsp groundnut or vegetable oil

50g (2oz) sweetened dried mango, roughly chopped

275ml (9fl oz) water

Authentic Indian breads, like naan and chapattis, contain minimal ingredients and are always flat, whether or not they contain any yeast. This bread is quite the opposite – well risen, intensely spiced and dispersed with nuggets of sweet dried mango. It makes an excellent alternative sandwich bread for chicken, cheese and salads. *Illustrated*

1 Crush the cardamom pods, using a pestle and mortar, until the shells are broken up. Pick out the shells and discard. Add the cumin and coriander seeds and crush the seeds until coarsely ground. Add the onion seeds, chilli flakes, turmeric and ginger, and mix together.

2 Put the ingredients into the bread maker bucket, following the order and method specified in the manual, adding the spices and dried mango with the flour.

3 Fit the bucket into the bread maker and set to the basic programme with a crust of your choice. Press start.

4 Just before baking, brush the top of the dough with water and scatter with black onion seeds.

5 After baking, remove the bread from the machine and shake out on to a wire rack to cool.

Beetroot and caraway loaf

MAKES 1 MEDIUM LOAF: ABOUT 10 SLICES

PER SLICE: 170 cals; 3g fat; 33g carbohydrate

1 tsp easy-blend dried yeast

400g (14oz) strong white bread flour

1 tsp salt

2 tsp caraway seeds

2 tsp golden caster sugar

25g (1oz) butter

275ml (9fl oz) beetroot juice

Sweet, earthy beetroot juice gives this spicy bread an incredibly vibrant colour and moist texture, making it an interesting choice for cheese, cold meat or roasted vegetable sandwiches. Buy natural beetroot juice or, better still, make your own using a juice extractor. You'll need 400g (14oz) fresh raw beetroot to extract sufficient juice.

1 Put the ingredients into the bread maker bucket, following the order and method specified in the manual.

2 Fit the bucket into the bread maker and set to the basic programme with a crust of your choice. Press start.

3 After baking, remove the bread from the machine and shake out on to a wire rack to cool.

Basil, Manchego and Serrano bread

MAKES 1 MEDIUM LOAF: ABOUT 10 SLICES

PER SLICE: 240 cals; 7g fat; 37g carbohydrate

1 tsp easy-blend dried yeast

475g (1lb 1oz) strong white bread flour

1 tsp salt

2 tsp golden caster sugar

2 tbsp extra-virgin olive oil

350ml (12fl oz) water

25g (1oz) fresh basil leaves, torn into pieces

100g (3½oz) Manchego cheese, diced

50g (2oz) Serrano ham, torn into small pieces

Like other cured meats, Serrano ham has an intense flavour, so a little goes a long way in a savoury loaf. Served warm in small chunks, this tasty bread is perfect with cold meats, olives and cheese, as a simple tapas style snack or starter. *Illustrated*

1 Put all the ingredients except the basil, cheese and ham into the bread maker bucket, following the order and method specified in the manual.

2 Fit the bucket into the bread maker and set to the basic programme with raisin setting, if applicable. Select the crust of your choice and press start. Add the basil, cheese and ham when the machine beeps, or halfway through the kneading cycle.

3 After baking, remove the bread from the machine and shake out on to a wire rack to cool.

Mushroom and garlic bread

MAKES 1 MEDIUM LOAF: ABOUT 10 SLICES

PER SLICE: 230 cals; 4g fat; 43g carbohydrate

40g (1½oz) dried mushrooms

200ml (7fl oz) boiling water

2 egg yolks

4 garlic cloves, thinly sliced

1 tsp easy-blend dried yeast

525g (1lb 3oz) strong white bread flour

1 tsp salt

2 tsp golden caster sugar

25g (1oz) butter

Dried mushrooms give this bread a superb depth of flavour. Choose from the wide variety now available – porcini, morels, chanterelles and shiitake all give good results – or use a bag of mixed dried mushrooms. A great bread for toasting and topping with scrambled or poached eggs, or for total indulgence fry slices in butter with bacon and tomatoes.

1 Soak the dried mushrooms in the boiling water for 15 minutes. Drain well, reserving the liquid. Set aside about 10 well shaped mushroom pieces for the topping. Make the reserved liquid up to 325ml (11fl oz) with cold water.

2 Put the ingredients into the bread maker bucket, following the order and method specified in the manual, adding the mushrooms after the flour.

3 Fit the bucket into the bread maker and set to the basic programme. Select the crust of your choice and press start.

4 Just before baking, scatter the reserved mushrooms over the surface of the bread.

5 After baking, remove the bread from the machine and shake out on to a wire rack to cool.

SAVOURY BREAD DOUGHS

FLOURY BAPS

GRAINY COTTAGE LOAF

PROVENÇAL BREAD RING

FRENCH COUNTRY BREAD

CIABATTA

FOCACCIA

FOCACCIA WITH SPINACH AND GORGONZOLA

RED ONION, SWEET POTATO AND GOAT'S CHEESE PIZZA

BASIL AND PINE NUT STROMBOLI

PARMESAN AND OLIVE GRISSINI

PEPPER AND PANCETTA BUNS

OLIVE PITTA BREADS

SPICED NAAN BREADS

CHORIZO AND PINE NUT MINI LOAVES

ROASTED RED ONION AND GRUYÈRE BREAD

GARLIC AND HERB ROLLS

HORSERADISH MUFFINS

GOAT'S CHEESE AND LOVAGE BUNS

Floury baps

MAKES 8 ROLLS

PER ROLL: 220 cals; 3g fat; 45g carbohydrate

1 tsp easy-blend dried yeast

450g (1 lb) strong white bread flour, plus extra to dust

1 tsp salt

1 tsp golden caster sugar

15g (½oz) butter

150ml (¼ pint) milk, plus extra to brush

125ml (4fl oz) water

These traditional Scottish breakfast rolls are made with milk and heavily dusted with flour to give a soft crumb and crust. Serve them warm, split and filled with anything from bacon and eggs to salad, cheese, cold meats or burgers.

1 Put the ingredients into the bread maker bucket, following the order and method specified in the manual.

2 Fit the bucket into the bread maker and set to the dough programme. Press start. Lightly grease a large baking sheet.

3 Once the dough is ready, turn it out on to a lightly floured surface and punch it down to deflate. Divide into 8 even sized pieces. Shape each piece into a round and flatten with the palm of your hand until about 10cm (4in) in diameter. Space slightly apart on the baking sheet and brush lightly with milk. Sprinkle generously with flour, cover loosely with a cloth and leave to rise for 30–40 minutes until doubled in size.

4 Preheat the oven to 200°C (180°C fan oven) mark 6. Make a deep impression in the centre of each bap with your thumb. Dust with a little more flour and bake for 18–20 minutes until risen and pale golden around the edges. Eat warm or transfer to a wire rack to cool.

French country bread

MAKES 1 LARGE LOAF: ABOUT 12 SLICES

PER SLICE: 170 cals; 3g fat; 34g carbohydrate

1½ tsp easy-blend dried yeast

300g (10oz) strong white bread flour, plus extra to dust

150g (5oz) spelt flour

50g (2oz) rye flour

1½ tsp salt

1 tbsp honey

25g (1oz) butter

350ml (12fl oz) milk

This lovely rustic loaf with its thick, floury crust and densely textured, golden crumb is great for lunches, sandwiches or toasting. It's best served fresh so if there's some left the day after baking, freeze it – ready sliced for convenience if you like.

1 Put the ingredients into the bread maker bucket, following the order and method specified in the manual.

2 Fit the bucket into the bread maker and set to the dough programme. Press start. Grease a large baking sheet.

3 Once the dough is ready, turn it out on to a floured surface and punch it down to deflate. Shape the dough into a ball and place on the baking sheet. Cover loosely with lightly oiled clingfilm and leave to rise in a warm place for about 30 minutes until doubled in size. Preheat the oven to 220°C (fan oven 200°C) mark 7.

4 Sprinkle the top of the dough with flour. Using a very sharp knife, make 4 or 5 deep cuts diagonally across the top of the dough, then similarly in the opposite direction to create a diamond pattern.

5 Bake for 15 minutes, then reduce the oven temperature to 190°C (fan oven 170°C) mark 5 and bake for a further 15–20 minutes or until the loaf sounds hollow when tapped underneath, covering with foil if it starts to brown too quickly. Transfer to a wire rack to cool.

Ciabatta

MAKES 2 LARGE CIABATTAS: EACH SERVES 4

PER SERVING: 250 cals; 4g fat; 48g carbohydrate

1 tsp easy-blend dried yeast

500g (1lb 2oz) strong white bread flour, plus extra to dust

1½ tsp salt

1 tsp golden caster sugar

2 tbsp olive oil

325ml (11fl oz) water

It is the high water content and lengthy rising that give an authentic ciabatta its aerated texture and irregular, slightly flattened shape. The bread machine makes a very acceptable version, eliminating the hassle of kneading a loose, sticky dough.

1 Put the ingredients into the bread maker bucket, following the order and method specified in the manual.

2 Fit the bucket into the bread maker and set to the dough programme. Press start. Oil a large baking sheet and sprinkle with flour.

3 Once the dough is ready, turn it out on to a well floured surface and cut in half, using a floured knife. Shape each piece of dough into a long strip and pass it from one hand to the other until it is stretched to about 28cm (11in) long. Lay the 2 dough strips well apart on the baking sheet. Leave to rise in a warm place, uncovered, for 30 minutes until doubled in size.

4 Preheat the oven to 220°C (fan oven 200°C) mark 7. Rub the dough lightly with a little extra flour to dust, then bake for 15–18 minutes until pale golden and crisp on the underside. Transfer to a wire rack to cool. Serve warm or cold.

Focaccia

MAKES 1 LARGE FOCACCIA: SERVES 8

PER SERVING: 280 cals; 9g fat; 45g carbohydrate

1 tsp easy-blend dried yeast
475g (1lb 1oz) strong white bread flour
1½ tsp salt
3 tbsp olive oil
300ml (½ pint) water

TO FINISH
Fresh rosemary sprigs
2 tbsp olive oil
Sea salt flakes

Focaccias come in many guises – soft or crisp, sprinkled with herbs, or piled lavishly with roasted vegetables. This recipe is a simple one, scattered with fragrant rosemary so the flavour permeates the dough. The flan ring helps the bread to rise and bake in a perfect round, but don't worry if you haven't got one, just lay the dough, pizza style, on the baking sheet.

1 Put the dough ingredients into the bread maker bucket, following the order and method specified in the manual.

2 Fit the bucket into the bread maker and set to the dough programme. Press start. Grease a 28cm (11in) metal flan ring and place on a greased baking sheet.

3 Once the dough is ready, turn it out on to a floured surface and punch it down to deflate. Roll out to a 25cm (10in) round and lay inside the flan ring, pushing the dough to the edges with your fingertips. (Don't worry if it shrinks back, the dough will expand to fill the ring as it proves.) Cover loosely with oiled clingfilm and leave to rise in a warm place for 30 minutes.

4 Using fingertips dipped in flour, make deep dimples all over the dough. Scatter with small rosemary sprigs, drizzle with the olive oil and sprinkle generously with sea salt flakes. Re-cover with oiled clingfilm and leave for a further 10 minutes, as the dough might have shrunk back when dimpled. Preheat the oven to 200°C (fan oven 180°C) mark 6.

5 Drizzle the dough with water. (This is not essential but helps the crust to stay soft during baking.) Bake for 20–25 minutes until just firm and pale golden. Transfer to a wire rack and leave to cool.

Basil and pine nut stromboli

MAKES 1 LOAF: ABOUT 10 SLICES

PER SLICE: 350 cals; 21g fat; 27g carbohydrate

1 tsp easy-blend dried yeast

350g (12oz) strong white bread flour

1 tsp salt

3 tbsp olive oil

200ml (7fl oz) water, plus 2 tbsp

FOR THE FILLING

1 tbsp olive oil

100g (3½oz) pine nuts

100g (3½oz) Parmesan cheese, freshly grated

200g (7oz) mozzarella cheese, finely chopped

25g (1oz) fresh basil leaves, torn into pieces

TO FINISH

1 tbsp olive oil

Sea salt flakes to sprinkle

This irresistible cheese bread is named after a tiny volcanic island near the foot of Italy, because the filling is meant to 'erupt' through a series of holes pierced in the dough before baking. Don't be put off if this doesn't happen with your version – it makes no difference to the flavour. The basic bread is similar to a focaccia dough, and the filling can be varied to taste. Try sun-dried tomatoes, roasted vegetables, cured ham or olives instead of the basil and pine nuts.

1 Put the dough ingredients into the bread maker bucket, following the order and method specified in the manual.

2 Fit the bucket into the bread maker and set to the dough programme. Press start.

3 While the dough is in the machine, prepare the filling. Heat the oil in a frying pan, add the pine nuts and fry for 2 minutes or until golden. Tip into a bowl and leave to cool slightly, then add the Parmesan, mozzarella and basil.

4 Preheat the oven to 200°C (180°C fan oven) mark 6. Lightly grease a large baking sheet.

5 Once the dough is ready, turn it out on to a lightly floured surface and punch it down to deflate. Cover with a tea-towel and leave to rest for 10 minutes, then roll out to a 35x25cm (14x10in) rectangle. Scatter with the filling to within 1cm (½in) of the edges. Loosely roll up the dough, starting from a short end, and transfer to the baking sheet so the join is underneath.

6 Cover the dough loosely with oiled clingfilm and leave in a warm place for 30 minutes until risen. Pierce the dough all over with a meat fork or large skewer, making sure you go right through to the baking sheet.

7 Drizzle with the olive oil and sprinkle with sea salt flakes. Bake for 30 minutes until risen and golden. Serve the bread warm, or transfer to a wire rack to cool.

Parmesan and olive grissini

MAKES 32

PER GRISSINI: 80 cals; 2g fat; 12g carbohydrate

1 tsp easy-blend dried yeast

500g (1lb 2oz) strong white bread flour

1 tsp salt

3 tbsp olive oil

2 tsp golden caster sugar

300ml (½ pint) water

50g (2oz) pitted black olives, finely chopped

50g (2oz) Parmesan cheese, freshly grated

TO FINISH

Semolina to dust

Beaten egg to glaze

Coarse salt flakes to sprinkle

These delicious breadsticks are a far cry from the dry, tasteless shop-bought variety. Flavoured with olives and Parmesan, they look and taste fantastic. Easy to digest and perfect for nibbling with antipasto, snacks or starters they will stimulate rather than curb the appetite. You can make them several days in advance and store in an airtight tin, popping them into a moderate oven for a couple of minutes before serving if they've softened slightly.

1 Put the dough ingredients into the bread maker bucket, following the order and method specified in the manual.

2 Fit the bucket into the bread maker and set to the dough programme with raisin setting, if applicable. Press start. Add the olives and Parmesan when the machine beeps or halfway through the kneading cycle. Lightly oil 2 large baking sheets and sprinkle with semolina.

3 Once the dough is ready, turn out on to a surface and punch it down to deflate. Cover with a tea-towel and leave to rest for 10 minutes.

4 Roll out the dough to a 30x20cm (12x8in) rectangle, cover loosely with a tea-towel and leave for 30 minutes until well risen. Preheat the oven to 220°C (fan oven 200°C) mark 7.

5 Cut the dough across the width into 4 thick bands. From each of these, cut 8 very thin strips and transfer them to the baking sheet, stretching each one until it is about 28cm (11in) long, and spacing the strips 1cm (½in) apart.

6 Brush very lightly with beaten egg and sprinkle with salt. Bake for 18–20 minutes until crisp and golden. Transfer to a wire rack to cool.

Pepper and pancetta buns

MAKES 12

PER BUN: 190 cals; 4g fat; 34g carbohydrate

2 tbsp chilli oil

2 red peppers, cored, deseeded and diced

1¼ tsp easy-blend dried yeast

500g (1lb 2oz) strong white bread flour

1 tsp salt

2 tsp golden caster sugar

3 tbsp sun-dried tomato paste

Several large fresh tarragon sprigs, roughly chopped

250ml (8fl oz) water

75g (3oz) sliced pancetta, torn into pieces

These intensely savoury little buns are packed with smoky pancetta, tarragon and red peppers that have been fried in chilli oil to accentuate their flavour. For practicality, they're baked inside little squares of parchment, so they're wrapped and ready to go in lunchboxes or picnic bags. They look stylish, too.

1 Heat the oil in a frying pan and fry the peppers for 4–5 minutes until soft. Cool slightly.

2 Put the remaining dough ingredients except the pancetta into the bread maker bucket, following the order and method specified in the manual, adding the tomato paste and tarragon with the water.

3 Fit the bucket into the bread maker and set to the dough programme with raisin setting, if applicable. Press start. Add the pancetta and peppers with any cooking juices when the machine beeps or halfway through the kneading cycle.

4 While the dough is proving, cut out twelve 14cm (5½in) squares of baking parchment and have ready a 12-section muffin or Yorkshire pudding tray.

5 Turn the dough out on to a floured surface and punch it down to deflate. Divide the dough into 12 even sized pieces. Push a square of parchment into one of the tin sections and drop a piece of dough into the centre. Repeat with the remainder. Cover loosely with a tea-towel and leave in a warm place for about 30 minutes until well risen. Preheat the oven to 220°C (fan oven 200°C) mark 7.

6 Bake the buns for 15–18 minutes until risen and golden. Lift the paper cases out of the tin sections and transfer to a wire rack to cool.

Olive pitta breads

MAKES 6

PER PITTA: 220 cals; 2g fat; 48g carbohydrate

½ tsp easy-blend dried yeast

375g (13oz) strong white bread flour, plus extra to dust

½ tsp salt

½ tsp ground cumin

½ tsp golden caster sugar

275ml (9fl oz) water

40g (1½oz) pitted black olives, finely chopped

Finely chopped olives and a dash of cumin give these pitta breads a special flavour. If you'd prefer a basic pitta recipe, simply leave out the olives and spice or, for wholemeal pittas, substitute half the white flour with strong wholemeal flour. All taste good – freshly baked or toasted.

1 Put all the ingredients except the olives into the bread maker bucket, following the order and method specified in the manual.

2 Fit the bucket into the bread maker and set to the dough programme with raisin setting, if applicable. Press start. Add the chopped olives when the machine beeps or halfway through the kneading cycle.

3 Once the dough is ready, turn it out on to a floured surface and punch it down to deflate. Cover with a tea-towel and leave for 10 minutes. Liberally dust a large baking sheet with flour. Preheat the oven to 220°C (fan oven 200°C) mark 7.

4 Divide the dough into 6 equal portions. Roll out each to an oval shape, about 22cm (8½in) long. Cover with a tea-towel and leave in a warm place for 20–25 minutes until beginning to rise.

5 Put the floured baking sheet into the oven for 5 minutes before baking to heat up. Lay the dough ovals on the baking sheet and bake for 5–8 minutes until golden. Wrap the pitta breads in a tea-towel to keep warm and retain their soft crust until ready to serve.

Spiced naan breads

MAKES 6

PER NAAN: 190 cals; 5g fat; 34g carbohydrate

2 tsp cumin seeds

1 tsp coriander seeds

1 tsp fennel seeds

¾ tsp easy-blend dried yeast

250g (9oz) strong white bread flour

¾ tsp salt

2 tsp caster sugar

1 tbsp vegetable oil

2 tbsp natural yogurt

125ml (4fl oz) water

15g (½oz) melted butter or ghee, to brush

Naan is one of the most popular leavened flat breads in India, particularly in the north where it is cooked in ferociously hot tandoor ovens, often alongside the meat it will be eaten with. A very hot grill works perfectly well for this authentic style naan that tastes so much fresher and better than bought imitations.

1 Lightly crush the cumin, coriander and fennel seeds, using a pestle and mortar.

2 Put the ingredients into the bread maker bucket, following the order and method specified in the manual, adding the spices with the flour.

3 Fit the bucket into the bread maker and set to the dough programme. Press start.

4 Once the dough is ready, turn in out on to a lightly floured surface and punch it down to deflate. Divide into 6 pieces and shape each into a ball. Roll out each one to a tear-drop shape, about 22cm (8½in) long and 12cm (5in) wide. Cover loosely with a cloth and leave for 20–30 minutes until beginning to puff up. Heat the grill to its highest setting.

5 You will probably need to cook the naan breads in 2 batches. Lay them on the hot grill pan and grill for about 3 minutes on each side until puffy and specked with brown spots. (Watch the bread quite closely as it will quickly begin to char). Brush lightly with butter or ghee and wrap in a clean towel to keep warm until ready to serve.

Chorizo and pine nut mini loaves

MAKES 8 INDIVIDUAL LOAVES

PER LOAF: 390 cals; 18g fat; 48g carbohydrate

3 tbsp olive oil

100g (3½oz) pine nuts

1 tbsp paprika

1½ tsp easy-blend dried yeast

475g (1lb 1oz) strong white bread flour

1 tsp salt

1 tbsp golden caster sugar

2 tsp dried oregano

275ml (9fl oz) water

125g (4oz) piece chorizo sausage, diced

Individual traditional shaped loaves look most attractive and single portion sized loaf tins are a good buy if you make lots of bread. They are available from good kitchen stores, but if you can't get hold of any, this recipe can be baked as one whole loaf. You will need to use a 900g (2lb) loaf tin and allow an extra 15–20 minutes in the oven.

1 Put the olive oil, pine nuts and paprika in a frying pan and fry gently for 3 minutes, stirring frequently. Remove the nuts with a slotted spoon and set aside, reserving the spiced oil.

2 Put all the remaining ingredients except the chorizo into the bread maker bucket, following the order and method specified in the manual, adding the oregano and flavoured oil with the water.

3 Fit the bucket into the bread maker and set to the dough programme with raisin setting, if applicable. Press start. Add the pine nuts and chorizo when the machine beeps or halfway through the kneading cycle. Grease eight 150ml (¼ pint) individual loaf tins.

4 Once the dough is ready, turn it out on to a floured surface and punch it down to deflate. Cut the dough into 8 even sized pieces. Roughly shape each into an oval and drop into a loaf tin. Cover loosely with oiled clingfilm and leave to rise in a warm place for 30 minutes until risen above the top of the tins. Preheat the oven to 200°C (fan oven 180°C) mark 6.

5 Place the tins on a baking sheet and bake for about 20 minutes until risen and golden. Shake the loaves out of the tins on to a wire rack to cool.

Roasted red onion and Gruyère bread

MAKES 1 ROUND BREAD: 6 LARGE WEDGES

PER WEDGE: 370 cals; 17g fat; 44g carbohydrate

2 tsp fennel seeds
1 tsp easy-blend dried yeast
300g (11oz) strong white bread flour
½ tsp celery salt
1 tsp golden caster sugar
2 tbsp olive oil
200ml (7fl oz) water

FOR THE TOPPING

3 tbsp olive oil
450g (1lb) red onions, thinly sliced
Several fresh thyme sprigs, chopped
100g (3½oz) Gruyère cheese, thinly sliced
Salt and freshly ground black pepper

This tasty bread is baked inside a flan ring, simply to give a neat round shape. If you do not have a suitable sized metal flan ring, simply roll the dough to a large round and place directly on the baking sheet.

1 Lightly crush the fennel seeds, using a pestle and mortar. Put all the dough ingredients into the bread maker bucket, following the order and method specified in the manual, adding the crushed fennel seeds with the flour.

2 Fit the bucket into the bread maker and set to the dough programme with pizza setting if available, if not then the dough setting. Press start.

3 While the dough is in the bread maker, prepare the topping. Heat the oil in a frying pan, add the onions and fry gently for about 10 minutes until golden, stirring frequently. Stir in the thyme and seasoning.

4 Place a 28cm (11in) round metal flan ring on a baking sheet. Brush the inside of the ring and baking sheet with oil.

5 Once the dough is ready, turn it out on to a floured surface, knead lightly and roll out to a 28cm (11in) round. Lift the dough round into the ring on the baking sheet. Arrange the fried onion and cheese slices over the surface to within 1cm (½in) of the edges. Cover loosely with oiled clingfilm and leave in a warm place for 20 minutes. Preheat the oven to 220°C (fan oven 200°C) mark 7.

6 Bake for 25–30 minutes until the crust is slightly risen and golden around the filling. Serve warm, cut into wedges.

Garlic and herb rolls

MAKES 10

PER ROLL: 270 cals; 13g fat; 31g carbohydrate

1 tsp easy-blend dried yeast

400g (14oz) strong white bread flour

1 tsp salt

1 tsp golden caster sugar

3 tbsp olive oil

300ml (10fl oz) water

FOR THE FILLING

4 garlic cloves, crushed

6 tbsp green pesto

1 tbsp olive oil

Salt and freshly ground black pepper

TO FINISH

Beaten egg, to glaze

1 tbsp olive oil

2 tbsp pine nuts, roughly chopped, to sprinkle

These are excellent if you are looking for quick and easy rolls to serve with soups or starters. The recipe uses garlicky pesto, but you could equally well substitute one of the other good ready-made pestos or pastes now available, such as roasted vegetable, or sun-dried tomato with garlic. Make the rolls on the day you intend to eat them, or freeze ahead for another time, warming them through before serving.

1 Put the dough ingredients into the bread maker bucket, following the order and method specified in the manual.

2 Fit the bucket into the bread maker and set to the dough programme. Press start.

3 While the dough is proving, make the filling. Mix together the garlic, pesto, olive oil and a little seasoning. Grease a large baking sheet.

4 Once the dough is ready, turn it out on to a floured surface and punch it down to deflate. Roll out the dough to a 28cm (11in) square and spread the filling to within 2cm (¾in) of one edge, and right to the edges on the other sides. Brush the uncovered edge with a little beaten egg.

5 Roll up the dough, starting from the side opposite the egg glazed one. Using a floured knife, cut the rolled dough into 10 even sized pieces and place the rolls, cut sides facing up, on the baking sheet, spacing them 3cm (1¼in) apart.

6 Cover loosely with oiled clingfilm and leave in a warm place to rise for 30–45 minutes until doubled in size. Preheat the oven to 220°C (fan oven 200°C) mark 7.

7 Brush the rolls with a little beaten egg to glaze and sprinkle with the pine nuts. Drizzle with the remaining olive oil. Bake for 15 minutes until risen and pale golden. Serve warm, or transfer to a wire rack to cool.

Horseradish muffins

MAKES 12

PER MUFFIN: 210 cals; 6g fat; 35g carbohydrate

1 large egg

225ml (7½fl oz) whole milk

50g (2oz) butter, melted

1½ tsp easy-blend dried yeast

500g (1lb 2oz) strong white bread flour

1½ tsp salt

3 tbsp grated hot horseradish, fresh or from a jar

2 tsp golden caster sugar

15g (½oz) rice flour

Oil to brush

Hot steaming muffins – crisp on the outside, yet spongy soft in the centre – are great for snacks right through the day. Serve them on their own, or filled with ham and eggs for a comforting lunch, breakfast or supper. Make plenty, so you can freeze leftovers for a later date. The rice flour isn't essential but it does give the muffins a lovely grainy crust.

1 Beat the egg, milk and butter together in a bowl, using a fork until evenly combined. Put all the ingredients except the rice flour into the bread maker bucket, following the order and method specified in the manual.

2 Fit the bucket into the bread maker and set to the dough programme. Press start.

3 Once the dough is ready, turn it out on to a lightly floured surface and punch it down to deflate. Divide the dough into 12 even sized pieces. Lightly grease a baking sheet.

4 Scatter the rice flour on to a plate. Shape each piece of dough into a ball and flatten slightly. Press both sides of each muffin gently in the rice flour to coat lightly. Transfer them to the baking sheet, spacing well apart.

5 Cover with lightly oiled clingfilm and leave to rise in a warm place until doubled in size, about 45 minutes.

6 Brush a large, heavy-based frying pan or griddle with a little oil. Using a fish slice, slide as many muffins into the pan as will fit comfortably and cook over a low heat for about 6–7 minutes on each side until deep golden and crisp. Keep warm while cooking the remainder. Serve split and lightly toasted.

Goat's cheese and lovage buns

MAKES 8 BUNS

PER BUN: 230 cals; 8g fat; 34g carbohydrate

1 tsp easy-blend dried yeast

350g (12oz) strong white bread flour

1 tsp salt

1 tsp freshly ground black pepper

2 tsp golden caster sugar

50g (2oz) butter

3 garlic cloves, sliced

Small handful of fresh lovage, scant 7g (¼oz), chopped

175ml (6fl oz) water

100g (3½oz) firm goat's cheese with rind

Milk to glaze

Ideal for picnics, these little buns are flavoured with lovage, plenty of black pepper and hidden pockets of goat's cheese. Used in moderation, fresh lovage has a warm, inviting flavour, rather like a strong, aromatic celery. If you cannot obtain it, substitute another intensely flavoured herb, like thyme, rosemary or sage.

1 Put all the ingredients except the cheese into the bread maker bucket, following the order and method specified in the manual, adding the garlic and lovage with the water.

2 Fit the bucket into the bread maker and set to the dough programme. Press start. Oil the base and sides of eight 125ml (4fl oz) dariole moulds or small terracotta flower pots. (Dust with flour if using flower pots.) Cut the cheese into small chunks.

3 Once the dough is ready, turn it out on to a floured surface and punch it down to deflate. Cut the dough into 8 even sized pieces and flatten slightly into thick rounds.

4 Take one piece and press several chunks of cheese into the centre. Bring the edges of the dough up around the cheese and pinch together to seal in the cheese. Roll the dough lightly between the palms of the hands to elongate it, then drop into a mould, with the pinched ends of the dough underneath. Repeat with the remainder.

5 Place on a baking sheet and cover loosely with oiled clingfilm. Leave in a warm place for about 30 minutes until the dough has risen well above the rims of the moulds. Preheat the oven to 200°C (fan oven 180°C) mark 6.

6 Brush the tops of the buns with a little milk and bake for 15–20 minutes until risen and golden. Loosen the buns and turn out of the moulds, transferring to a wire rack to cool.

4

SWEET ENRICHED BREADS

BOSTON BREAD

POPPY SEED AND ORANGE LOAF

SOUR CHERRY AND COCONUT LOAF

STEM GINGER AND PEAR BREAD

PECAN AND MAPLE LOAF

BLUEBERRY AND VANILLA BREAD

MALTED FRUIT LOAF

RYE AND RAISIN BREAD

HOT CROSS BUN LOAF

SWEET SAFFRON CAKE

PIGNOLA

PISTACHIO SPICE BREAD

CHOCOLATE MACADAMIA LOAF

TROPICAL FRUIT AND RUM LOAF

Boston bread

MAKES 1 SMALL LOAF: ABOUT 10 SLICES

PER SLICE: 190 cals; 1g fat; 40g carbohydrate

1¼ tsp easy-blend dried yeast

175g (6oz) strong wholemeal bread flour

150g (5oz) strong white bread flour

50g (2oz) rye flour

50g (2oz) cornmeal

1 tsp salt

5 tbsp molasses or black treacle

250ml (8fl oz) milk

50g (2oz) raisins

Traditionally Boston bread is baked in a tall, round container and therefore resembles an Italian panettone. This version looks more like a conventional loaf and has an irresistibly warm, rich crumb. Although the bread is sweetened with molasses and raisins, it is good served with spicy stews, soups and bean dishes – to mop up the tasty juices. *Illustrated*

1 Put all the ingredients except the raisins into the bread maker bucket, following the order and method specified in the manual, adding the cornmeal with the flours.
2 Fit the bucket into the bread maker and set to the basic programme, or the recommended programme for mixed grain breads. Select a light crust and press start. Add the raisins when the machine beeps or halfway through the kneading cycle.
3 After baking, remove the bread from the machine and shake out on to a wire rack to cool.

Poppy seed and orange loaf

MAKES 1 MEDIUM LOAF: ABOUT 10 SLICES

PER SLICE: 240 cals; 9g fat; 41g carbohydrate

4 tbsp poppy seeds

Grated zest and juice of 2 oranges

1 tsp easy-blend dried yeast

400g (14oz) strong white bread flour

50g (2oz) medium oatmeal

½ tsp salt

50g (2oz) golden caster sugar

50g (2oz) butter

2 large eggs

This is a mildly flavoured, airy bread that lends itself more to breakfast than teatime. It is particularly good toasted and buttered. The poppy seeds are toasted to enhance their nutty flavour, which marries well with the gentle tang of the oranges.

1 Put the poppy seeds in a small frying pan and heat gently until the seeds are lightly toasted, about 3 minutes. Remove from the heat.
2 Make the orange juice up to 175ml (6fl oz) with water. (If the oranges are very juicy you might not need any water). Add the orange zest.
3 Put the ingredients into the bread maker bucket, following the order and method specified in the manual, adding the toasted poppy seeds with the flour.
4 Fit the bucket into the machine and set to the basic programme. Select a light crust and press start.
5 After baking, remove the bread from the machine and shake out on to a wire rack to cool.

Sour cherry and coconut loaf

MAKES 1 SMALL LOAF: ABOUT 10 SLICES

PER SLICE: 310 cals; 11g fat; 47g carbohydrate

1¼ tsp easy-blend dried yeast

425g (15oz) strong white bread flour

½ tsp salt

50g (2oz) golden caster sugar

40g (1½oz) butter

2 tsp almond extract

100g (3½oz) creamed coconut, chilled and grated

300ml (½ pint) milk

75g (3oz) dried sour cherries

Icing sugar to dust

Because of its high fat content, creamed coconut gives this bread a slightly cakey texture – dense and crumbly, with a spongy crust. Dried sour cherries provide a wonderful, tangy flavour but dried cranberries, raisins or sultanas can be used instead. *Illustrated*

1 Put all the ingredients except the cherries into the bread maker bucket, following the order and method specified in the manual, adding the creamed coconut with the flour.

2 Fit the bucket into the machine and set to the basic programme with raisin setting, if applicable. Select a light crust and press start. Add the dried cherries when the machine beeps or halfway through the kneading cycle.

3 After baking, remove the bread from the machine and shake out on to a wire rack to cool. Serve lightly dusted with icing sugar.

Stem ginger and pear bread

MAKES 1 SMALL LOAF: ABOUT 10 SLICES

PER SLICE: 210 cals; 3g fat; 42g carbohydrate

125g (4oz) dried pears

4 pieces preserved stem ginger, from a jar

1 tsp easy-blend dried yeast

400g (14oz) strong white bread flour

½ tsp salt

25g (1oz) light muscovado sugar

25g (1oz) butter

3 tbsp skimmed milk powder

275ml (9fl oz) water

3 tbsp stem ginger syrup to glaze

Dried pears and stem ginger in syrup add plenty of flavour and sweetness to this light, white loaf. Other dried fruits, such as apricots or prunes, can be substituted for the pears if you can't find them.

1 Thinly slice 40g (1½oz) of the pears and reserve for the topping. Roughly chop the remainder. Finely chop the stem ginger.

2 Put the remaining ingredients into the bread maker bucket, following the order and method specified in the manual.

3 Fit the bucket into the machine and set to the basic programme with raisin setting, if applicable. Select a light crust and press start. Add the chopped ginger and pears when the machine beeps or halfway through the kneading cycle.

4 Just before baking, brush along the middle of the loaf with water and arrange the sliced pears in a line to decorate.

5 After baking, remove the bread from the machine and shake out on to a wire rack to cool. Brush with the ginger syrup to glaze.

Pecan and maple loaf

MAKES 1 MEDIUM LOAF: ABOUT 10 SLICES

PER SLICE: 300 cals; 13g fat; 43g carbohydrate

100g (3½oz) pecan nuts

1¼ tsp easy-blend dried yeast

400g (14oz) strong white bread flour

½ tsp salt

1 tsp ground cinnamon

4 tbsp sunflower or groundnut oil

25g (1oz) dark muscovado sugar

100ml (3½fl oz) maple syrup

150ml (¼ pint) water

Milk to brush

4 tbsp maple syrup to glaze

Richly flavoured with chopped nuts, maple syrup and cinnamon, this sweet bread is perfect with a cup of coffee at any time of the day, and is especially good toasted. If you can't get pecan nuts, use walnuts instead.

1 Roughly chop the pecan nuts. Put all the remaining ingredients into the bread maker bucket, following the order and method specified in the machine, adding the maple syrup with the water.

2 Fit the bucket into the machine and set to the basic programme with raisin setting, if applicable. Select a light crust and press start. Add two-thirds of the chopped nuts when the machine beeps or halfway through the kneading cycle.

3 Just before baking, brush the surface of the dough with milk and scatter with the remaining nuts.

4 After baking, remove the bread from the machine and shake out on to a wire rack to cool. Brush with the maple syrup while still warm.

Blueberry and vanilla bread

MAKES 1 SMALL LOAF: ABOUT 10 SLICES

PER SLICE: 190 cals; 3g fat; 38g carbohydrate

1 tsp easy-blend dried yeast

400g (14oz) strong white bread flour

½ tsp salt

50g (2oz) golden caster sugar

25g (1oz) butter

3 tbsp skimmed milk powder

4 tsp vanilla extract

275ml (9fl oz) water

100g (3½oz) semi-dried blueberries

Try to find semi-dried blueberries for this recipe. Resembling currants, they are really juicy and sweet, and release plenty of flavour into the dough. The amount of vanilla may seem excessive, but it's not overpowering in the finished bread. Be sure to use natural vanilla extract, not the synthetic vanilla flavouring that is widely available.

1 Put all the ingredients except the blueberries into the bread maker bucket, following the order and method specified in the manual.

2 Fit the bucket into the bread maker and set to the basic programme with raisin setting, if applicable. Select a light crust and press start. Add the blueberries when the machine beeps or halfway through the kneading cycle.

3 After baking, remove the bread from the machine and shake out on to a wire rack to cool.

Malted fruit loaf

MAKES 1 MEDIUM LOAF: ABOUT 10 SLICES

PER SLICE: 280 cals; 5g fat; 55g carbohydrate

1½ tsp easy-blend dried yeast

400g (14oz) strong white bread flour

100g (3½oz) strong brown bread flour

1 tsp salt

50g (2oz) dark muscovado sugar

50g (2oz) butter

3 tbsp skimmed milk powder

3 tbsp malt extract

300ml (½ pint) water

125g (4oz) raisins

Icing sugar to dust

Malt extract gives bread a lovely soft texture and sweet, homemade flavour. Lightly specked with fruit, this loaf is not too rich and can easily be spiced up with a teaspoon of cinnamon or ground ginger if you like.

1 Put all the ingredients except the raisins into the bread maker bucket, adding the malt extract with the water.

2 Fit the bucket into the bread maker and set to the basic programme with raisin setting, if applicable. Select a light crust and press start. Add the raisins when the machine beeps or halfway through the kneading cycle.

3 After baking, remove the bread from the machine and shake out on to a wire rack to cool. Dust with icing sugar.

Rye and raisin bread

MAKES 1 MEDIUM LOAF: ABOUT 10 SLICES

PER SLICE: 250 cals; 5g fat; 47g carbohydrate

1¼ tsp easy-blend dried yeast

250g (9oz) strong white bread flour

200g (7oz) rye flour, plus extra to dust

½ tsp salt

50g (2oz) butter

50g (2oz) dark muscovado sugar

3 tbsp milk powder

250ml (9fl oz) water

75g (3oz) raisins

Like all rye breads this one has a dense texture and distinctively tangy flavour. It's not overly sweet, so it is good topped with preserve, or you can serve it simply buttered. Don't expect the top of the loaf to dome in the centre – it might even dip slightly, as is normal with rye breads.

1 Put all the ingredients except the raisins into the bread maker bucket, following the order and method specified in the manual.

2 Fit the bucket into the bread maker and set to the basic programme with raisin setting, if applicable. Select a light crust and press start. Add the raisins when the machine beeps or halfway through the kneading cycle.

3 Just before baking starts, lightly brush the top of the dough with water and sprinkle with rye flour.

4 After baking, remove the bread from the machine and shake out on to a wire rack to cool.

Hot cross bun loaf

MAKES 1 MEDIUM LOAF: ABOUT 10 SLICES

PER SLICE: 280 cals; 3g fat; 59g carbohydrate

1½ tsp easy-blend dried yeast

450g (1lb) strong white bread flour

½ tsp salt

2 tsp ground mixed spice

1 tsp ground ginger

50g (2oz) dark muscovado sugar

25g (1oz) butter

Finely grated zest of 1 lemon

275ml (9fl oz) milk

225g (8oz) luxury mixed dried fruit

TO FINISH

25g (1oz) plain flour

2 tbsp water

2 tbsp golden syrup

This large spicy, moist and fruity loaf is the quick and easy alternative hot cross bun. It saves you the trouble of shaping, proving and finishing a dozen smaller ones. The flavour is just as good and the slices can be toasted and buttered – just like traditional buns. *Illustrated*

1 Put all the ingredients except the dried fruit into the bread maker bucket, adding the lemon zest with the milk.
2 Fit the bucket into the bread maker and set to the basic programme with raisin setting, if applicable. Select a light crust and press start. Add the fruit when the machine beeps or halfway through the kneading cycle.
3 When the bread starts to bake, put the plain flour in a small bowl and gradually beat in the 2 tbsp water to make a thick paste, adding a dash more water if necessary. Spoon into a small, strong polythene bag and squeeze the paste into one corner. Snip off a small tip so the paste can be piped from the bag.
4 When the bread has about 30 minutes baking time left, raise the lid and pipe a flour paste cross on top of the loaf.
5 After baking, remove the bread from the machine and shake out on to a wire rack to cool. Brush the top with golden syrup to glaze.

Sweet saffron cake

MAKES 1 MEDIUM LOAF: ABOUT 10 SLICES

PER SLICE: 260 cals; 7g fat; 43g carbohydrate

½ tsp saffron threads, lightly crushed

150ml (¼ pint) water

1¼ tsp easy-blend dried yeast

350g (12oz) strong white bread flour

½ tsp salt

3 tbsp milk powder

1 large egg

75g (3oz) unsalted butter, melted

125g (4oz) luxury mixed dried fruit

100g (3½oz) no-soak dried prunes, chopped

2 tbsp clear honey to glaze

Saffron is a traditional ingredient in sweet, yeasted doughs and marries well with dried fruits. Saffron threads aren't easy to measure, but if you buy them from the supermarket in small jars you'll need about half a sachet.

1 Put the saffron in a cup, pour on 2 tbsp boiling water and leave to stand for 5 minutes. Add the infused liquid to the measured water.
2 Put all the ingredients except the dried fruit into the bread maker bucket, following the order and method specified in the manual.
3 Fit the bucket into the machine and set to the basic programme with raisin setting, if applicable. Select a light crust and press start. Add the fruit when the machine beeps or halfway through the kneading cycle.
4 After baking, remove the bread from the machine and shake out on to a wire rack to cool. Brush the top of the loaf with the honey to glaze.

Pignola

MAKES 1 MEDIUM LOAF: ABOUT 10 SLICES

PER SLICE: 290 cals; 11g fat; 42g carbohydrate

50g (2oz) pine nuts

50g (2oz) flaked almonds

1¼ tsp easy-blend dried yeast

400g (14oz) strong white bread flour

¾ tsp salt

2 tbsp golden caster sugar

50g (2oz) butter

1 large egg

3 tbsp skimmed milk powder

Finely grated zest of 2 oranges

225ml (7½fl oz) water

75g (3oz) sultanas

Beaten egg to glaze

Icing sugar to dust

Toasted pine nuts, almonds, sultanas and orange zest give this Italian fruit bread plenty of flavour and texture. It's light enough for breakfast, but good with coffee or tea at any time. *Illustrated*

1 Put the pine nuts and flaked almonds in a frying pan over a low heat and toast lightly for about 3 minutes, shaking the pan frequently. Tip on to a plate and set aside.

2 Put all the remaining ingredients except the sultanas into the bread maker bucket, adding the orange zest with the water.

3 Fit the bucket into the bread maker and set to the basic programme with raisin setting, if applicable. Select a light crust and press start. Add the sultanas and all but 3 tbsp of the toasted nuts when the machine beeps or halfway through the kneading cycle.

4 Just before baking, brush the surface of the bread with beaten egg and scatter with the reserved nuts.

5 After baking, remove the bread from the machine and shake out on to a wire rack to cool. Dust with icing sugar.

Pistachio spice bread

MAKES 1 MEDIUM LOAF: ABOUT 10 SLICES

PER SLICE: 430 cals; 21g fat; 53g carbohydrate

1¼ tsp easy-blend dried yeast

450g (1lb) strong white bread flour

½ tsp salt

2 tsp ground cinnamon

1 tsp ground ginger

3 tbsp milk powder

75g (3oz) unsalted butter, melted

25g (1oz) golden caster sugar

100ml (3½fl oz) orange flower water

75g (3oz) clear honey

75g (3oz) unsalted butter, melted

100ml (3½fl oz) water

100g (3½oz) pistachio nuts, roughly chopped

50g (2oz) blanched almonds, roughly chopped

Icing sugar to dust

A delicious blend of pistachio nuts, cinnamon, ginger and orange flower water give this loaf a slightly exotic flavour that sets it apart from other sweet breads. It's quite a firm textured bread that's best eaten fresh, or perked up in the toaster a day later.

1 Put all the ingredients except the nuts into the bread maker bucket, following the order and method specified in the manual, adding the orange flower water and honey with the water.

2 Fit the bucket into the bread maker and set to the basic programme with raisin setting, if applicable. Select a light crust and press start. Add the nuts when the machine beeps or halfway through the kneading cycle.

3 After baking, remove the bread from the machine and shake out on to a wire rack to cool. Dust liberally with icing sugar to finish.

Chocolate macadamia loaf

MAKES 1 MEDIUM LOAF: ABOUT 10 SLICES

PER SLICE: 450 cals; 25g fat; 52g carbohydrate

100g (3½oz) macadamia nuts, roughly chopped

1 large egg, plus 2 egg yolks

75g (3oz) unsalted butter, melted

2 tsp finely chopped fresh rosemary

175ml (6fl oz) water

1¼ tsp easy-blend dried yeast

400g (14oz) strong white bread flour

¾ tsp salt

50g (2oz) golden caster sugar

75g (3oz) plain chocolate, chopped

175g (6oz) white chocolate, chopped

This subtly flavoured loaf is an excellent choice for a late, leisurely breakfast. *Illustrated*

1 Lightly toast the nuts in a frying pan over a low heat for about 3 minutes, shaking the pan frequently. Tip on to a plate and set aside.

2 Mix together the egg, egg yolks, butter, rosemary and water. Put all the ingredients except the nuts and chocolate into the bread maker bucket, following the order and method specified in the manual.

3 Fit the bucket into the machine and set to the basic programme with raisin setting, if applicable. Select a light crust and press start. Add the nuts, plain chocolate and 125g (4oz) of the white chocolate when the machine beeps or halfway through the kneading programme.

4 After baking, remove the bread from the machine and shake out on to a wire rack to cool. Once the bread has cooled, melt the remaining white chocolate carefully in a bowl over a pan of hot water, stir until smooth and spread over the top of the loaf. Leave to set.

Tropical fruit and rum loaf

MAKES 1 SMALL LOAF: ABOUT 10 SLICES

PER SLICE: 260 cals; 3g fat; 50g carbohydrate

125g (4oz) dried tropical fruits, roughly chopped

50g (2oz) sultanas

3 tbsp rum

1 tsp easy-blend dried yeast

375g (13oz) strong white bread flour

½ tsp salt

25g (1oz) dark muscovado sugar

1 large egg

25g (1oz) butter

2 pieces preserved stem ginger from a jar, chopped, plus
  2 tbsp syrup

175ml (6fl oz) water

TO GLAZE

3–4 tsp rum

75g (3oz) golden icing sugar

Dried tropical fruits are widely available in mixed packs, containing mango, papaya, pineapple, etc; you can use any combination here. The fruits are added during kneading so they stay in chunky pieces.

1 Put the tropical fruits, sultanas and rum in a small bowl, cover and leave to stand for 1 hour, turning the fruits occasionally.

2 Put all the remaining dough ingredients into the bread maker bucket, following the order and method specified in the manual, adding the chopped ginger and syrup with the water.

3 Fit the bucket into the bread maker and set to the basic programme with raisin setting, if applicable. Select a light crust and press start. Add the tropical fruit mixture and any unabsorbed rum when the machine beeps or halfway through the kneading cycle.

4 After baking, remove the bread from the machine and shake out on to a wire rack to cool. In a small bowl, beat 3 tsp rum with the icing sugar until smooth and the consistency of thick pouring cream, adding a little more rum if necessary. Spoon the icing over the bread, letting it run down the sides. Leave to set.

Sticky currant buns

MAKES 8

PER BUN: 250 cals; 3g fat; 53g carbohydrate

1 tsp easy-blend dried yeast
350g (12oz) strong white bread flour
½ tsp salt
1 tsp ground mixed spice
15g (½oz) butter
Finely grated zest of 1 orange
25g (1oz) light muscovado sugar
200ml (7fl oz) milk
75g (3oz) currants

TO FINISH

25g (1oz) light muscovado sugar
2 tbsp water
50g (2oz) rough sugar pieces, lightly crushed

It's the rough, craggy appearance of these fruit buns that makes them so inviting, so don't waste time rolling and shaping them carefully. They are delicious served warm from the oven, split and buttered, or if a day or two old, try them toasted.

1 Put all the dough ingredients except the currants into the bread maker bucket, following the order and method specified in the manual.
2 Fit the bucket into the bread maker and set to the dough programme with raisin setting, if applicable. Add the currants when the machine beeps or halfway through the kneading cycle. Lightly grease a large baking sheet.
3 Once the dough is ready, turn out on to a floured surface and punch it down to deflate. Divide into 8 even sized pieces, scrunch into rounds and space slightly apart on the baking sheet. Cover with oiled clingfilm and leave to rise in a warm place for 30 minutes until doubled in size. Preheat the oven to 220°C (fan oven 200°C) mark 7.
4 Bake the buns for 10–15 minutes until golden. Meanwhile put the muscovado sugar in a small pan with the 2 tbsp water and heat gently until the sugar dissolves.
5 Transfer the buns to a wire rack and brush with the glaze, sprinkling them with the crushed sugar as you work. Leave to cool.

Sweet tea buns

MAKES 8

PER BUN: 280 cals; 4g fat; 57g carbohydrate

1 tsp easy-blend dried yeast
475g (1lb 1oz) strong white bread flour
¼ tsp salt
15g (½oz) butter
75g (3oz) golden caster sugar
1 tsp vanilla extract
1 large egg
225ml (7½fl oz) milk
Icing sugar to dust

TO SERVE

Whipped double cream or clotted cream
Strawberry conserve

These simple, sweet, doughy buns are best treated rather like scones. Serve them split and topped with whipped or clotted cream, and spoonfuls of strawberry preserve.

1 Put the ingredients into the bread maker bucket, following the order and method specified in the manual.
2 Fit the bucket into the bread maker and set to the dough programme. Press start. Grease a large baking sheet.
3 Once the dough is ready, turn out on to a floured surface and punch it down to deflate. Divide into 8 even sized pieces. Shape each piece into a ball and place on the baking sheet, spacing them at least 3cm (1¼in) apart. Cover loosely with oiled clingfilm and leave to rise in a warm place for about 30 minutes until doubled in size. Preheat the oven to 220°C (fan oven 200°C) mark 7.
4 Bake the buns for about 12 minutes until risen and pale golden. Lift on to a wire rack and dust generously with icing sugar. Leave to cool. Serve with whipped or clotted cream and strawberry conserve.

Fruit and spice teacakes

MAKES 10

PER TEACAKE: 270 cals; 5g fat; 52g carbohydrate

1½ tsp easy-blend dried yeast
400g (14oz) strong white bread flour
50g (2oz) strong wholemeal bread flour
½ tsp salt
1 tsp ground cinnamon
½ tsp ground allspice
75g (3oz) dark muscovado sugar
40g (1½oz) unsalted butter, diced
300ml (½ pint) whole milk
140g (4½oz) mixed dried fruit

Unlike most of those that you buy, these teacakes are packed with flavour, mildly spiced and irresistibly more-ish, particularly if you serve them lightly toasted and lavished with melting butter.

1 Put all the ingredients except the dried fruit in the bread maker bucket, following the order and method specified in the manual.
2 Fit the bucket into the bread maker and set to the dough programme with raisin setting, if applicable. Press start. Add the mixed dried fruit when the machine beeps or towards the end of the kneading cycle. Grease a large baking sheet.
3 Once the dough is ready, turn out on to a floured surface and punch it down to deflate. Cut the dough into 10 even sized pieces and shape each into a ball. Place on the baking sheet, spacing them slightly apart, and cover loosely with oiled clingfilm. Leave to rise in a warm place for about 30 minutes until doubled in size. Preheat the oven to 220°C (fan oven 200°C) mark 7.
4 Bake the buns for about 20 minutes until risen and deep golden. Transfer to a wire rack to cool. Serve split and toasted.

Doughnuts with clotted cream and jam

MAKES 10

PER DOUGHNUT: 280 cals; 11g fat; 40g carbohydrate

1 tsp easy-blend dried yeast

450g (1lb) strong white bread flour

1 tsp salt

50g (2oz) caster sugar

1 tsp vanilla extract

1 large egg

25g (1oz) unsalted butter, diced

225ml (7½fl oz) whole milk

Oil for deep-frying

TO SERVE

Golden caster sugar to sprinkle

Strawberry or raspberry conserve

Clotted cream or extra-thick double cream

Bought doughnuts, however fresh, will simply never taste the same again once you've sampled these delights. Rather than fiddling to fill the dough with piped jam, the doughnuts are served with spoonfuls of strawberry or raspberry conserve and clotted cream. Unlike many classic recipes that are updated to make them more modern, healthy and light, these doughnuts are totally indulgent ... spoil yourself!

1 Put the dough ingredients into the bread maker bucket, following the order and method specified in the manual.

2 Fit the bucket into the bread maker and set to the dough programme. Press start. Grease a large baking sheet.

3 Once the dough is ready, turn out on to a floured surface and punch it down to deflate. Divide into 10 equal sized pieces. Roll each piece into a ball and space well apart on the baking sheet. Cover loosely with oiled clingfilm and leave to rise in a warm place for 30–40 minutes until doubled in size.

4 Heat a 5cm (2in) depth of oil in a large, heavy-based saucepan or deep fryer until a scrap of dough dropped into the oil sizzles and browns in 30 seconds. Add as many doughnuts as will fit comfortably in the pan and fry for 2–3 minutes until golden, reducing the heat if they brown too quickly. Remove from the pan with a slotted spoon and leave to drain on kitchen paper, while you fry the remainder.

5 Toss the doughnuts in plenty of caster sugar while still warm. Serve with strawberry or raspberry conserve and clotted cream.

Lemon glazed Chelsea buns

MAKES 12

PER BUN: 310 cals; 8g fat; 56g carbohydrate

1 large egg
50g (2oz) unsalted butter, melted
225ml (7½fl oz) whole milk
1½ tsp easy-blend dried yeast
400g (14oz) strong white bread flour
100g (3½oz) strong softgrain or Granary flour
1 tsp salt
75g (3oz) light muscovado sugar

FOR THE FILLING AND TOPPING

2 pieces stem ginger from a jar, plus 3 tbsp syrup
100g (3½oz) raisins
100g (3½oz) sultanas
50g (2oz) light muscovado sugar
2 tsp ground mixed spice
Finely grated zest and juice of 1 lemon
40g (1½oz) unsalted butter, in pieces

Good home-made Chelsea buns are well worth the effort. These sweet swirls of indulgent dough encase a sugary blend of dried fruits and stem ginger. Like most fruity breads, they are best eaten warm, so if you make them ahead, pop them in the oven for a few minutes before serving.

1 In a bowl, whisk the egg, butter and milk together with a fork. Put all the dough ingredients into the bread maker bucket, following the order and method specified in the manual.

2 Fit the bucket into the bread maker and set to the dough programme. Press start.

3 Grease a 23cm (9in) square cake tin, 7.5cm (3in) deep. For the filling, finely chop the stem ginger and mix in a bowl with the raisins, sultanas, 25g (1oz) of the sugar, the spice and lemon zest.

4 Once the dough is ready, turn out on to a floured surface and punch it down to deflate. Roll out to a 30cm (12in) square and spread with the filling to within 1cm (½in) of the edges. Dot with the butter. Roll up the dough to enclose the filling, then cut into 2.5cm (1in) thick slices.

5 Pack the slices, cut sides uppermost, into the greased cake tin, spacing them evenly apart. Cover with oiled clingfilm and leave to rise in a warm place for about 45 minutes until doubled in size and rising up towards the top of the tin. Preheat the oven to 200°C (fan oven 180°C) mark 6.

6 Bake the buns for 20 minutes, then lower the oven setting to 180°C (fan oven 160°C) mark 4 and bake for a further 5–10 minutes until risen and deep golden. In the meantime, mix together the remaining sugar, lemon juice and stem ginger syrup to make a glaze. Transfer the buns to a wire rack and brush with the glaze. Leave to cool.

Pandolce

MAKES 1 LARGE LOAF: ABOUT 12 SLICES

PER SLICE: 270 cals; 6g fat; 51g carbohydrate

1 tsp easy-blend dried yeast

500g (1lb 2oz) strong white bread flour

½ tsp salt

100g (3½oz) golden caster sugar

50g (2oz) butter, melted

1 large egg

Finely grated zest of 1 lemon

2 tsp vanilla extract

200ml (7fl oz) water

150g (5oz) candied peel, finely chopped

50g (2oz) chopped mixed nuts

Icing sugar to dust (optional)

This is similar to Italian panettone, but without all the dried fruit. Candied peel provides the predominant flavour, so it's important to use good quality peel and chop it yourself, rather than resort to the ready chopped variety from the supermarkets. Like panettone, leftovers freeze well and make a great bread and butter pudding.

1 Put all the ingredients except the candied peel and nuts into the bread maker bucket, following the order and method specified in the manual, adding the lemon zest and vanilla with the water.

2 Fit the bucket into the bread maker and set to the dough programme with raisin setting, if applicable. Press start. Add the candied peel and nuts when the machine beeps or halfway through the kneading cycle. Grease a 15cm (6in) round cake tin, 9cm (3½in) deep, and line with a triple thickness strip of baking parchment, to extend 5cm (2in) above the rim of the tin.

3 Once the dough is ready, turn out on to a floured surface and punch it down to deflate. Shape into a ball and drop it into the tin. Cover loosely with a tea-towel and leave to rise in a warm place for about 45 minutes or until the dough reaches the top of the paper lining. Preheat the oven to 200°C (fan oven 180°C) mark 6.

4 Bake for 30–35 minutes until risen and deep golden, covering with foil if the top appears to be browning too quickly. Shake the bread out on to a wire rack and tap the bottom – it should sound hollow. If not return to the oven for a little longer. Leave on the wire rack to cool and dust with icing sugar before serving if you like.

Traditional brioche

MAKES 1 SMALL LOAF: ABOUT 10 SLICES

PER SLICE: 140 cals; 6g fat; 20g carbohydrate

1 tsp easy-blend dried yeast

225g (8oz) strong white bread flour

¼ tsp salt

25g (1oz) golden caster sugar

2 large eggs, beaten

50g (2oz) butter, melted

Beaten egg to glaze

Because of the high proportion of butter and eggs, French brioche is almost sponge-like in texture with a rich, golden colour. No water is used in the dough; eggs and melted butter are simply added to the bread machine as other liquids would be normally.

1 Put the ingredients into the bread maker bucket, following the order and method specified in the manual.

2 Fit the bucket into the bread maker and set to the dough programme. Press start. Oil a 1 litre (1¾ pint) fluted brioche mould, or a 900g (2lb) loaf tin if you do not have a traditional brioche mould.

3 Once the dough is ready, turn out on to a floured surface and punch it down to deflate. Shape three-quarters of the dough into a ball and drop into the mould. Push a small crater into the top of the ball, using floured fingers. Shape the remaining dough into a small ball and press gently into the indented top. (If using a loaf tin, put the dough into the tin in one piece.)

4 Cover loosely with oiled clingfilm and leave in a warm place to rise for about 45 minutes until doubled in size. Preheat the oven to 220°C (fan oven 200°C) mark 7.

5 Brush the dough with beaten egg to glaze and bake for about 20–25 minutes until golden and firm, covering with foil if the top appears to be browning too quickly. Shake the brioche out of the mould and transfer to a wire rack to cool.

Honey, lemon and pine nut brioche

MAKES 1 SMALL LOAF: ABOUT 10 SLICES

PER SLICE: 230 cals; 12g fat; 26g carbohydrate

100g (3½oz) pine nuts, lightly toasted

50g (2oz) demerara sugar

Finely grated zest of 1 lemon

1 tbsp lemon juice

1 tsp easy-blend dried yeast

225g (8oz) strong white bread flour

¼ tsp salt

3 tbsp clear honey

2 large eggs, beaten

40g (1½oz) butter

TO FINISH

Milk to glaze

3 tbsp clear honey

2 tbsp lemon juice

Like the traditional brioche, this recipe is light, sweet and buttery, but it also has pockets of sugary pine nuts layered in the dough. After baking, the brioche is drizzled with a tangy lemon honey glaze that seeps into the bread for extra flavour.

1 In a bowl, mix together the toasted pine nuts, sugar, lemon zest and juice. Set aside.

2 Put the remaining ingredients into the bread maker bucket, following the order and method specified in the manual. (The melted butter and eggs are the only liquid ingredients in this recipe). Set to the dough programme and press start. Grease a 450g (1lb) loaf tin and line with baking parchment.

3 Once the dough is ready, turn out on to a floured surface and punch it down to deflate. Divide into 3 pieces and pull or roll each into a rectangle, slightly larger than the base of the tin.

4 Fit one rectangle into the tin and scatter with a third of the pine nut mixture. Cover with a second dough rectangle and scatter with half the remaining pine nut mixture. Position the other sheet of dough on top. Brush with a little milk and scatter with the remaining pine nut mixture.

5 Cover loosely with oiled clingfilm and leave to rise in a warm place for about 45 minutes until the dough has risen to about 2cm (¾in) above the rim of the tin. Preheat the oven to 200°C (fan oven 180°C) mark 6.

6 Put the bread in the oven, positioning a baking sheet on the shelf below to catch any nuts that fall from the surface. Bake for 25 minutes, covering the bread with foil if it appears to be browning too quickly.

7 Meanwhile, mix together the honey and lemon juice. Remove the bread from the oven and make plenty of large holes all over the surface, using a skewer. Drizzle the glaze over the holes so that most of it is absorbed into the bread. Leave to cool.

Fig, lemon and cardamom plait

MAKES 1 LARGE LOAF: ABOUT 12 THICK SLICES

PER SLICE: 380 cals; 13g fat; 61g carbohydrate

1½ tsp easy-blend dried yeast

400g (14oz) strong white bread flour

100g (3½oz) strong wholemeal bread flour

1 tsp salt

50g (2oz) golden caster sugar

40g (1½oz) unsalted butter, diced

325ml (11fl oz) whole milk

FOR THE FILLING

250g (9oz) dried figs

Finely grated zest of 2 lemons

1 tbsp lemon juice

100g (3½oz) brazil nuts, coarsely chopped

25g (1oz) golden caster sugar

50g (2oz) unsalted butter, diced

FOR THE ICING

2 tsp cardamom pods

125g (4oz) icing sugar

2 tbsp lemon juice

Plaited sweet and savoury breads look clever, but they do take a little more effort than any other shaped breads. Here figs and lemon are a perfect partnership, but you might prefer to substitute another dried fruit, such as raisins, apricots or dates.

1 Put the dough ingredients into the bread maker bucket, following the order and method specified in the manual.

2 Fit the bucket into the bread maker and set to the dough programme. Press start.

3 While the dough is in the bread maker, prepare the filling. Chop the figs into small pieces and mix with the lemon zest and juice, nuts, caster sugar and butter. Grease a large baking sheet.

4 Once the dough is ready, turn out on to a floured surface and punch it down to deflate. Divide into 3 equal pieces. Roll out each piece to a 35x12cm (14x5in) strip. Don't worry about squaring up the corners. Spoon the filling down each strip to within 1cm (½in) of the edges, level out evenly, then press down lightly into the dough. Roll up the dough pieces to make 3 long, thick sausages, enclosing the filling.

5 Lay the strips in parallel lines with the joins on the underside. Pinch the pieces together at one end, then plait the strips and tuck the ends underneath. Transfer to the baking sheet.

6 Cover loosely with oiled clingfilm and leave to rise in a warm place for about 30 minutes or until doubled in size. Preheat the oven to 200°C (fan oven 180°C) mark 6.

7 Bake the plait for 25 minutes until it is risen and golden, and sounds hollow when tapped underneath.

8 In the meantime, make the glaze. Crack the cardamom pods using a pestle and mortar to release the seeds, pick out the shells, then crush the seeds as finely as possible. Put them in a bowl with the icing sugar and 4–5 tsp lemon juice. Mix to a paste, the consistency of thick pouring cream, adding another 1 tsp lemon juice if necessary. Transfer the plait to a wire rack and spoon over the icing. Leave to cool.

Chunky chocolate and hazelnut loaf

MAKES 1 MEDIUM LOAF: ABOUT 8 THICK SLICES

PER SLICE: 380 cals; 21g fat; 42g carbohydrate

2 egg yolks

25g (1oz) unsalted butter, melted

125ml (4fl oz) whole milk

100g (3½oz) unblanched hazelnuts

¾ tsp easy-blend dried yeast

225g (8oz) strong white bread flour

¼ tsp salt

25g (1oz) golden caster sugar

FOR THE FILLING

175g (6oz) plain chocolate, broken into pieces

50g (2oz) unsalted butter, diced

TO FINISH

Golden caster sugar to dust

Oozing pockets of rich melting chocolate and chunky hazelnuts, this gorgeous bread is a chocolate lover's dream! Ideally, it is best eaten about an hour after baking, so it's cool enough to slice but the chocolate is still melted. If you do make it ahead, wrap in foil and warm through in the oven until the chocolate melts again.

1 Whisk the egg yolks, butter and milk together in a bowl, using a fork. Roughly chop the hazelnuts, set aside half for the filling and finely chop the remainder.

2 Put the dough ingredients into the bread maker bucket, following the order and method specified in the manual, adding the finely chopped nuts after the flour.

3 Fit the bucket into the bread maker and set to the dough programme. Press start. Grease and lightly flour a 900g (2lb) loaf tin.

4 Once the dough is ready, turn out on to a floured surface and punch it down to deflate. Take a third of the dough and roll it out on a floured surface to a rectangle, large enough to line the base and two-thirds of the way up the sides of the tin. Lift the dough into the tin, pressing it into the corners to make a case. Cut the remaining dough roughly into 20 pieces.

5 Scatter a few pieces of chocolate, nuts and butter over the base of the dough. Scatter with a third of the dough pieces, then add more chocolate, nut and butter pieces so they fall between the dough. Continue piling up the dough and filling until used up, making sure the last of the chocolate is packed down between the last of the dough.

6 Cover loosely with oiled clingfilm and leave to rise in a warm place for about 45 minutes until the dough comes just above the top of the tin. Preheat the oven to 200°C (fan oven 180°C) mark 6.

7 Bake for 15 minutes, then reduce the oven temperature to 180°C (fan oven 160°C) mark 4 and bake for a further 15 minutes until risen and golden. Leave to cool in the tin for 10 minutes, then transfer to a wire rack to cool. Serve dusted with sugar.

Marzipan and ginger kugelhopf

MAKES 1 LARGE KUGELHOPF: 12 THICK SLICES

PER SLICE: 320 cals; 11g fat; 47g carbohydrate

1 large egg
75g (3oz) unsalted butter
150ml (¼ pint) freshly squeezed orange juice
1 tsp easy-blend dried yeast
375g (13oz) strong white bread flour
½ tsp salt
50g (2oz) golden caster sugar

FOR THE FILLING

50g (2oz) piece fresh root ginger, peeled and finely grated
100g (3½oz) sultanas
250g (9oz) white almond paste, coarsely grated
4 tbsp Cointreau or other orange liqueur
Finely grated zest and juice of ½ lemon

TO FINISH

Icing sugar to dust

Marzipan, sultanas and fresh ginger, spiked with a little orange liqueur, makes a scrumptious filling with a decidedly festive flavour. For a traditional shape, you need a fluted, ring kugelhopf mould, but if you haven't got one, you can use a standard 1.5 litre (2½ pint) ring tin, or simply shape a free-form dough ring on a baking sheet, sealing the ends together well. When you put the dough ingredients in the bread maker, pop the almond paste in the freezer to firm up and you will find it much easier to grate.

1 Whisk the egg, butter and orange juice together in a bowl, using a fork. Put the dough ingredients into the bread maker bucket, following the order and method specified in the manual.

2 Fit the bucket into the bread maker and set to the dough programme. Press start. Thoroughly grease and flour the base and sides of a 1.5 litre (2½ pint) kugelhopf tin.

3 Once the dough is ready, turn out on to a floured surface and punch it down to deflate. Roll out the dough to a 35x25cm (14x10in) rectangle. Scatter with the ginger, sultanas and almond paste, taking the filling to 1cm (½in) from the edges. Sprinkle with the orange liqueur, lemon zest and juice.

4 Starting from a long edge, loosely roll up the dough. With the join uppermost, quickly lift the roll into the tin, bringing the ends round to meet each other with no gaps.

5 Cover loosely with oiled clingfilm and leave to rise in a warm place until the dough comes just above the rim of the tin, about 1–1¼ hours. (The dough will be slow to rise because of its high butter and sugar content.) Preheat the oven to 200°C (fan oven 180°C) mark 6.

6 Bake the kugelhopf for 35–40 minutes until risen and deep golden. Leave in the tin for 10 minutes, then loosen the top edges with a knife. Invert on to a wire rack and leave to cool. (If the bread has risen unevenly, slice off the top to level it before turning out.) Serve dusted with icing sugar.

Cinnamon and ginger swirl

MAKES 1 MEDIUM LOAF: ABOUT 10 SLICES

PER SLICE: 240 cals; 8g fat; 38g carbohydrate

50g (2oz) unsalted butter, melted

1 large egg

150ml (¼ pint) milk

1 tsp easy-blend dried yeast

375g (13oz) strong white bread flour

½ tsp salt

65g (2½oz) light muscovado sugar

TO FINISH

2 tsp ground cinnamon

½ tsp ground allspice

25g (1oz) demerara sugar, plus extra to sprinkle

25g (1oz) unsalted butter

50g (2oz) fresh root ginger, peeled

Milk to brush

This easy bread looks deceptively clever when sliced into. It makes a great breakfast bread, served warm or toasted, preferably spread with butter or a little orange marmalade.

1 In a bowl, beat the butter with the egg and milk until evenly combined. Put all the dough ingredients into the bread maker bucket, following the order and method specified in the manual.

2 Fit the bucket into the bread maker and set to the dough programme. Press start.

3 Grease a 900g (2lb) loaf tin. For the filling, mix together the cinnamon, allspice and demerara sugar.

4 Once the dough is ready, turn out on to a floured surface and punch it down to deflate. Roll out to a rectangle 33cm (13in) long and make the width of the dough the same as the length of the prepared loaf tin.

5 Brush right up to the edges of the dough with the melted butter and sprinkle with the spice mix. Grate the ginger directly over the spices, distributing it as evenly as possible. Starting from a short end, roll up the dough and fit into the tin with the join underneath.

6 Cover loosely with oiled clingfilm and leave to rise in a warm place for about 1 hour until risen above the top of the tin. Preheat the oven to 200°C (fan oven 180°C) mark 6.

7 Brush the top of the dough with a little milk and sprinkle with extra demerara sugar. Bake for about 30 minutes until risen and deep golden, covering with foil if the crust appears to be browning too quickly. Remove from the tin and transfer to a wire rack to cool.

Pistachio and rosewater stollen

MAKES 1 STOLLEN: ABOUT 10 THICK SLICES

PER SLICE: 380 cals; 17g fat; 51g carbohydrate

1¼ tsp easy-blend dried yeast

350g (12oz) strong white bread flour

½ tsp salt

1 tsp ground mixed spice

25g (1oz) golden caster sugar

50g (2oz) butter, melted

150ml (¼ pint) milk

3 tbsp rosewater

75g (3oz) sultanas

50g (2oz) pistachio nuts

50g (2oz) candied peel, chopped

FOR THE MARZIPAN

150g (5oz) pistachio nuts, skinned

40g (1½oz) golden caster sugar

40g (1½oz) golden icing sugar

2 egg yolks

TO FINISH

Icing sugar to dust

Stollen is a German Christmas bread that's packed with festive fruit and nuts, and is often given as a present. This version has a dense, but deliciously sweet, nutty texture, and slicing it reveals a filling of pistachio marzipan. For a vibrantly coloured marzipan it's best to skin the pistachios first, by soaking them in boiling water for a couple of minutes then rubbing between pieces of kitchen paper to remove the skins.

1 Put all the dough ingredients except the sultanas, pistachio nuts and candied peel into the bread maker bucket, following the order and method specified in the manual.

2 Fit the bucket into the bread maker and set to the dough programme with raisin setting, if applicable. Press start. Add the sultanas, pistachio nuts and candied peel when the machine beeps or halfway through the kneading cycle.

3 Meanwhile make the marzipan. Put the pistachio nuts in a food processor and blend until finely ground. Add the sugars and egg yolks and blend to a paste. Turn out on to the work surface and shape into a log, 24cm (9½in) long. Grease a large baking sheet.

4 Once the dough is ready, turn out on to a floured surface and punch it down to deflate. Roll out to an oblong, 28cm (11in) long and 15cm (6in) wide. Lay the marzipan on the dough, slightly to one side of the centre. Brush the long edges of the dough with water then fold the wider piece of dough over the paste, sealing well.

5 Transfer to the baking sheet, cover loosely with oiled clingfilm and leave in a warm place for about 40 minutes until doubled in size. Preheat the oven to 200°C (fan oven 180°C) mark 6.

6 Bake for 20–25 minutes until risen and golden. Transfer to a wire rack to cool. Serve lavishly dusted with icing sugar.

Redcurrant schiacciata

MAKES 1 SCHIACCIATA: ABOUT 10 WEDGES

PER WEDGE: 310 cals; 15g fat; 39g carbohydrate

¾ tsp easy-blend dried yeast

350g (12oz) strong white bread flour

¼ tsp salt

2 tbsp olive oil

2 tbsp golden caster sugar

6 tbsp sherry or Marsala

150ml (¼ pint) water

FOR THE TOPPING

200g (7oz) cream cheese

Finely grated zest and juice of 1 small orange

Finely grated zest and juice of ½ lemon

1 tsp vanilla extract

3 tbsp double cream

50g (2oz) icing sugar, plus extra to dust

250g (9oz) redcurrants

For this Italian dessert 'pizza,' the light dough is rolled, spread with flavoured cream cheese and scattered with redcurrants. This schiacciata cuts into plenty of wedges, so it's ideal for a large gathering. To enjoy it at its best, serve on the day it is made.

1 Put the dough ingredients into the bread maker bucket, following the order and method specified in the manual, adding the sherry or Marsala with the water.

2 Fit the bucket into the bread maker and set to the dough programme with pizza setting if available, if not then the dough setting. Press start.

3 While proving, make the topping. Beat the cream cheese in a bowl to soften. Gradually beat in the orange and lemon zest and juice, vanilla extract, cream and icing sugar. Grease a large baking sheet.

4 When the dough is ready, turn it out on to a floured surface and roll out to a 30cm (12in) round. Transfer to the baking sheet and spread to within 1cm (½in) of the edges with the cream cheese mixture. Cover loosely with oiled clingfilm and leave to rise in a warm place for 30 minutes until risen around the edges.

5 Scatter with the redcurrants and dust lavishly with icing sugar. Bake for 25–30 minutes until the dough is risen and golden. Dust with a little more icing sugar and serve warm or cold.

6

GLUTEN-FREE BREADS

Basic gluten-free white bread

MAKES 1 SMALL LOAF: ABOUT 10 THICK SLICES

PER SLICE: 130 cals; 2g fat; 27g carbohydrate

1 tsp easy-blend dried yeast

350g (12oz) gluten-free bread flour, for bread machines

½ tsp salt

1 tbsp olive oil

300ml (½ pint) water

A useful 'all-rounder' for anyone on a gluten-free diet, this bread is equally good freshly sliced for sandwiches and snacks, or toasted. Like all the breads in this chapter it can be frozen (sliced first for convenience), and it makes good breadcrumbs for other dishes too.

1 Put the ingredients into the bread maker bucket, following the order and method specified in the manual.

2 Fit the bucket into the bread maker and set to the programme and crust recommended for gluten-free breads. Press start.

3 After baking, remove the bread from the machine and shake out on to a wire rack to cool.

Chunky seed loaf

MAKES 1 SMALL LOAF: ABOUT 10 THICK SLICES

PER SLICE: 160 cals; 6g fat; 26g carbohydrate

2 tbsp sesame seeds

1 tbsp poppy seeds

1 tbsp pumpkin seeds

1 tbsp linseeds

1 tsp easy-blend dried yeast

350g (12oz) gluten-free fibre mix, for bread machines

½ tsp salt

2 tsp light muscovado sugar

15g (½oz) butter

325ml (11fl oz) water

Packed with healthy seeds, this loaf is made with gluten-free fibre mix to give a texture that resembles a traditional brown loaf. Fibre mixes are based on the same gluten-free wheat starch as standard gluten-free flour, with added vegetable fibre. As they usually absorb more water, you need to check the mixture during the kneading cycle, adding a dash more water if necessary. This seeded loaf is a great breakfast bread to toast and lavish with butter and marmalade. *Illustrated*

1 Mix the seeds together and reserve 1 tbsp to sprinkle. Put all the ingredients into the bread maker bucket, following the order and method specified in the manual, adding the seeds with the flour.

2 Fit the bucket into the bread maker and set to the programme and crust recommended for gluten-free breads. Press start.

3 Just before baking starts, scatter the reserved seeds over the surface of the dough.

4 After baking, remove the bread from the machine and shake out on to a wire rack to cool.

Sun-dried tomato and herb loaf

MAKES 1 SMALL LOAF: ABOUT 10 THICK SLICES

PER SLICE: 150 cals; 3g fat; 30g carbohydrate

Small handful of fresh herbs, about 15g (½oz)

1 tsp easy-blend dried yeast

350g (12oz) gluten-free bread flour, for bread machines

½ tsp salt

1 tbsp golden caster sugar

25g (1oz) butter

4 tbsp sun-dried tomato paste

300ml (½ pint) water

You can use a handful of almost any fresh herb in this bread. Thyme, parsley, fennel and tarragon are all sufficiently intense, while rosemary and oregano go particularly well with the sun-dried tomato flavour. *Illustrated*

1 Reserve several of the herb sprigs for garnish; finely chop the rest, discarding any tough stalks. Put the ingredients into the bread maker bucket, following the order and method specified in the manual, adding the chopped herbs and tomato paste with the water.

2 Fit the bucket into the bread maker and set to the programme and crust recommended for gluten-free breads. Press start.

3 Just before baking, scatter the reserved herb sprigs over the surface of the dough.

4 After baking, remove the bread from the machine and shake out on to a wire rack to cool.

Parmesan and pancetta bread

MAKES 1 SMALL LOAF: ABOUT 10 THICK SLICES

PER SLICE: 190 cals; 5g fat; 32g carbohydrate

2 tbsp olive oil

50g (2oz) pancetta, finely chopped

25g (1oz) Parmesan cheese, freshly grated

1¼ tsp easy-blend dried yeast

400g (14oz) gluten-free bread flour, for bread machines

¼ tsp salt

1 tsp golden caster sugar

325ml (11fl oz) water

Italian pancetta has a tempting aroma and sweet, spicy flavour. Most supermarkets now stock it, either thinly sliced or in small dice. If you can't find any, use finely chopped smoked streaky bacon instead.

1 Heat the olive oil in a small frying pan, add the pancetta and fry for 2–3 minutes until beginning to colour. Cool slightly.

2 Reserve 1 tbsp of the Parmesan cheese to sprinkle. Put all the remaining ingredients into the bread maker bucket, adding the pancetta (plus the oil from the pan) and cheese with the water.

3 Fit the bucket into the bread maker and set to the programme and crust recommended for gluten-free breads. Press start.

4 Just before baking, scatter the reserved cheese over the surface of the dough.

5 After baking, remove the bread from the machine and shake out on to a wire rack to cool.

Roasted vegetable bread

MAKES 1 SMALL LOAF: 10 THICK SLICES

PER SLICE: 160 cals; 3g fat; 39g carbohydrate

75g (3oz) dried vegetables, such as aubergine, tomatoes,
  courgettes, mushrooms
boiling water to soak (see method)
1 tsp easy-blend dried yeast
350g (12oz) gluten-free bread flour, for bread machines
½ tsp celery salt
2 tbsp olive oil

Small packs of dried vegetables, usually roasted, are now widely available and well worth buying to make tasty savoury breads in the bread machine. They have a more intense flavour than fresh vegetables, so a little goes a long way. This bread is great for sandwiches, or serving with soups and antipasto-style starters.

1 Put the dried vegetables into a small bowl and add enough boiling water to just cover them. Leave for 20 minutes or until the vegetables are softened. Drain thoroughly, reserving the liquid, and chop the vegetables into small pieces. Make the liquid up to 300ml (½ pint) with cold water if necessary. If the water is still hot, leave until tepid.

2 Put all the ingredients into the bread maker bucket, following the order and method specified in the manual, adding the chopped vegetables with the water.

3 Fit the bucket into the bread machine and set to the programme and crust recommended for gluten-free breads. Press start.

4 After baking, remove the bread from the machine and shake out on to a wire rack to cool.

Chilli spiced bread

MAKES 1 MEDIUM LOAF: ABOUT 12 SLICES

PER SLICE: 150 cals; 3g fat; 29g carbohydrate

12 cardamom pods
2 tsp cumin seeds
2 tsp black onion seeds
½ tsp dried chilli flakes
½ tsp ground turmeric
1¼ tsp easy-blend dried yeast
400g (14oz) gluten-free bread flour, for bread machines
½ tsp salt
1 tsp golden caster sugar
2 tbsp groundnut or vegetable oil
40g (1½oz) sultanas
325ml (11fl oz) water

This spicy, seeded bread is great with Indian dishes as an alternative to the more usual naan or poppadums, or even just to liven up a lunchtime sandwich. Other dried or semi-dried fruits like apricots, peaches or mango can be used instead of sultanas, or you can leave them out altogether for a less sweet flavour.

1 Crush the cardamom pods, using a pestle and mortar, until the shells are broken up. Pick out the shells and discard. Add the cumin seeds and crush lightly. Stir in the onion seeds, chilli flakes and turmeric.
2 Put all the ingredients into the bread maker bucket, following the order and method specified in the manual, adding the crushed seeds and sultanas with the water.
3 Fit the bucket into the bread maker and set to the programme and crust recommended for gluten-free breads. Press start.
4 After baking, remove the bread from the machine and shake out on to a wire rack to cool.

Caramelised onion and olive bread

MAKES 1 MEDIUM LOAF: ABOUT 12 SLICES

PER SLICE: 160 cals; 4g fat; 28g carbohydrate

2 small red onions, 200g (7oz) in total, thinly sliced
3 tbsp olive oil
1 tsp golden caster sugar
1¼ tsp easy-blend dried yeast
400g (14oz) gluten-free bread flour, for bread machines
½ tsp salt
1 tbsp chopped thyme, preferably lemon thyme
25g (1oz) pitted black olives, sliced
325ml (11fl oz) water

The secret of this bread is to caramelise the onions until they are really sweet before adding them to the bread machine. Lemon thyme gives a lovely, fresh bite, but you can use ordinary thyme or flavour the bread with a different fresh herb if you prefer.

1 Put the onions in a heavy-based frying pan with 2 tbsp of the oil and the sugar. Fry gently for 8–10 minutes until caramelised, stirring frequently. Cool for 5 minutes.
2 Put all the ingredients into the bread maker bucket, following the order and method specified in the manual, adding the onions, remaining oil, thyme and olives with the water.
3 Fit the bucket into the bread maker and set to the programme and crust recommended for gluten-free breads. Press start.
4 After baking, remove the bread from the machine and shake out on to a wire rack to cool.

Spiced fruit and nut loaf

MAKES 1 MEDIUM LOAF: ABOUT 12 SLICES

PER SLICE: 170 cals; 2g fat; 36g carbohydrate

100g (3½oz) luxury mixed dried fruit

350ml (12fl oz) hot strong tea

1 tsp easy-blend dried yeast

375g (13oz) gluten-free fibre mix, for bread machines

½ tsp salt

50g (2oz) dark muscovado sugar

2 tsp ground mixed spice

25g (1oz) butter

3 pieces stem ginger from a jar, chopped, plus 2 tbsp
    syrup

Richly flavoured with preserved stem ginger and mixed spice, this teabread is excellent sliced and buttered. Allow about an hour for the dried fruit to steep in the hot tea before you make the loaf. *Illustrated*

1 Put the dried fruit into a bowl, pour on the hot tea and leave to steep for 1 hour.

2 Tip the fruit and tea into the bread maker bucket. Add all the remaining ingredients except the ginger syrup, following the order and method specified in the manual, adding the chopped ginger with the tea.

3 Fit the bucket into the bread maker and set to the programme and crust recommended for gluten-free breads. Press start.

4 After baking, remove the bread from the machine and shake out on to a wire rack to cool. While still warm, brush the top of the loaf with the stem ginger syrup to glaze.

Sweet cider bread

MAKES 1 SMALL LOAF: ABOUT 10 THICK SLICES

PER SLICE: 170 cals; 2g fat; 34g carbohydrate

300ml (½ pint) medium cider

1 tsp easy-blend dried yeast

350g (12oz) gluten-free bread flour, for bread machines

¼ tsp salt

1 tbsp golden caster sugar

15g (½oz) butter

75g (3oz) dried pears, chopped

1 tsp ground cinnamon

Icing sugar to dust

Dried pears and cinnamon are a good flavour combination in this teabread. If dried pears aren't available, use another dried fruit instead, such as apricots, prunes, peaches or pineapple.

1 Measure the cider and let it stand for 20–30 minutes to go flat. Put the ingredients into the bread maker bucket, following the order and method specified in the manual, adding the chopped pears and cinnamon with the cider.

2 Fit the bucket into the bread machine and set to the programme and crust recommended for gluten-free breads. Press start.

3 After baking, remove the bread from the machine and shake out on to a wire rack to cool. Serve dusted liberally with icing sugar.

7

CAKES AND TEABREADS

CRANBERRY MUFFIN CAKE

STICKY GINGERBREAD

CHOCOLATE, BANANA AND CINNAMON TEABREAD

CARDAMOM AND ORANGE CAKE

FRESH GINGER AND MARMALADE CAKE

RASPBERRY AND OATMEAL CAKE

GOOSEBERRY AND ALMOND MADEIRA

SPICY CARROT CAKE

CHOCOLATE FRUIT AND NUT CAKE

COCONUT CREAM CAKE

ESPRESSO AND WALNUT CAKE

LAVENDER AND LEMON CAKE

Cranberry muffin cake

MAKES 8 SLICES

PER SLICE: 330 cals; 12g fat; 54g carbohydrate

100g (3½oz) unsalted butter, melted
200ml (7fl oz) milk
1 large egg
finely grated zest of 1 orange
275g (10oz) plain flour
2 tsp baking powder
150g (5oz) golden caster sugar, plus extra to sprinkle
75g (3oz) dried sweetened cranberries

This crumbly textured, tangy cranberry loaf is best served really fresh – preferably warm and topped with a dot of butter. To vary the taste, use dried blueberries or cherries in place of cranberries.

1 Grease and line the bread maker bucket with baking parchment, if specified in the manual. In a bowl, beat together the butter, milk, egg and orange zest.

2 Sift the flour and baking powder together into a large bowl. Stir in the sugar and dried cranberries. Fold in the milk mix, using a large metal spoon, until the mixture is only just combined. Turn into the bread maker bucket and level the surface.

3 Fit the bucket into the bread maker and set to the cake or bake only programme. Select 50 minutes on the timer and choose a light crust. Press start.

4 To check whether the cake is cooked, pierce the centre with a skewer; it should come out fairly clean. If necessary re-set the timer for a little longer.

5 Remove the bucket from the machine and turn the cake out on to a wire rack to cool. Sprinkle generously with caster sugar. Serve the muffin cake sliced and buttered.

Sticky gingerbread

MAKES 10 SLICES

PER SLICE: 350 cals; 11g fat; 56g carbohydrate

115g (4oz) unsalted butter

115g (4oz) light muscovado sugar

75g (3oz) black treacle

200g (7oz) golden syrup

250g (9oz) plain flour

2 tsp ground mixed spice

65g (2½oz) stem ginger from a jar, finely chopped

2 large eggs

100ml (3½fl oz) milk

1 tsp bicarbonate of soda

2 tbsp hot water

Extra treacle or golden syrup to glaze (optional)

This is a traditional gingerbread – sweet, dark, spicy and soft – best served with lingering warmth. It also keeps well, wrapped and stored in an airtight container for up to a week.

1 Put the butter, sugar, treacle and golden syrup in a saucepan and heat gently until the butter has melted. Leave to cool for 5 minutes. Grease and line the bread maker bucket with baking parchment, if specified in the manual.

2 Sift the flour and mixed spice together into a bowl. Add the syrup mixture, chopped ginger, eggs and milk, and stir well until combined.

3 In a cup, mix the bicarbonate of soda with the hot water, then add to the bowl. Stir the mixture well and pour into the bread maker bucket.

4 Fit the bucket into the bread maker and set to the cake or bake only programme. Select 1 hour 10 minutes on the timer and choose a light crust. Press start.

5 To check whether the cake is done, pierce the centre with a skewer; it should come out fairly clean. If necessary, re set the timer for a little longer.

6 Remove the bucket from the machine, leave the cake in it for 5 minutes, then transfer to a wire rack. Brush the top of the cake with the treacle or syrup to glaze if preferred and leave to cool.

Chocolate, banana and cinnamon teabread

MAKES 10 SLICES

PER SLICE: 330 cals; 17g fat; 42g carbohydrate

3 medium bananas
100g (3½oz) chocolate, in pieces
1 tsp ground cinnamon
150g (5oz) unsalted butter, softened
125g (4½oz) light muscovado sugar
2 large eggs
225g (8oz) self-raising flour
1 tsp baking powder
1 tbsp milk

This recipe is ideal for using up over-ripe bananas that are past their best for eating. Indeed, they will give a better result than less ripe fruit. Slicing into the moist teabread reveals enticing layers of spicy chocolate sauce.

1 Grease and line the bread maker bucket with baking parchment, if specified in the manual. Mash the bananas in a bowl, using a fork.

2 Put the chocolate, cinnamon and 25g (1oz) of the butter in a separate bowl over a pan of gently simmering water and leave until melted, stirring occasionally.

3 Put the remaining butter, sugar, eggs, flour and baking powder into another bowl and beat with an electric whisk for about 2 minutes until smooth and creamy. Stir in the milk and mashed bananas.

4 Spoon a third of the banana mixture into the bucket and spread to an even layer. Spoon half of the chocolate mixture on top, spreading it gently to the edges. Repeat these layers, then cover with the remaining cake mixture.

5 Fit the bucket into the bread maker and set to the cake or bake only programme. Select 1 hour on the timer and choose a light crust. Press start.

6 To check whether the cake is done, press the surface with your hand; it should feel firm. If necessary, re-set the timer and cook a little longer.

7 Remove the bucket from the machine, leave the cake in it for 10 minutes, then transfer to a wire rack to cool.

Cardamom and orange cake

MAKES 12 SLICES

PER SLICE: 340 cals; 18g fat; 43g carbohydrate

2 tsp cardamom pods
175g (6oz) unsalted butter, softened
175g (6oz) light muscovado sugar, plus extra to sprinkle
finely grated zest and juice of 1 orange
250g (9oz) luxury mixed dried fruit
100g (3½oz) ground almonds
2 large eggs
200g (7oz) plain flour
1 tsp baking powder

Cardamom gives an interesting twist to this light fruit cake, but it can be omitted if preferred.

1 Grease and line the bread bucket with baking parchment, if specified in the manual. Crush the cardamom pods, using a pestle and mortar, until the shells break up. Pick out the shells, then lightly crush the seeds.
2 Beat the butter and sugar together in a bowl until creamy. Add the orange zest and juice, dried fruit, ground almonds, crushed cardamom seeds and eggs, and beat until well mixed.
3 Sift the flour and baking powder into the bowl and fold the ingredients together until combined. Turn into the bucket and level the surface.
4 Fit into the bread maker and set to the cake or bake only programme. Select 1 hour on the timer and choose a light crust. Press start.
5 To check if the cake is done, pierce the centre with a skewer; it should come out fairly clean. If necessary re-set the timer for a little longer.
6 Remove the bucket from the machine, leave the cake in it for 10 minutes, then transfer to a wire rack. Sprinkle with sugar and let cool.

Fresh ginger and marmalade cake

MAKES 10 SLICES

PER SLICE: 370 cals; 22g fat; 37g carbohydrate

100g (3½oz) blanched almonds
175g (6oz) unsalted butter, softened
75g (3oz) fine demerara sugar
100g (3½oz) orange marmalade
3 large eggs
250g (9oz) self-raising flour
1 tsp baking powder
50g (2oz) piece fresh root ginger, peeled and grated
3 tbsp orange marmalade, warmed, to glaze

Either fine or course-cut marmalade can be used here for a tangy, fruity flavour. Serve the cake warm, with spoonfuls of mascarpone for an indulgent treat.

1 Whizz the almonds in a food processor until finely ground. Grease and line the bread bucket with baking parchment, if specified in the manual.
2 Put the butter, sugar and marmalade in a bowl and beat well until pale and creamy. Add the eggs, flour, baking powder, grated ginger and ground almonds and beat well until combined.
3 Turn the mixture into the bucket and level the surface. Fit the bucket into bread maker and set to the cake or bake only programme. Select 1 hour on the timer and choose a light crust. Press start.
4 To check if the cake is done, pierce the centre with a skewer; it should come out fairly clean. If necessary, re-set the timer for a little longer.
5 Remove the cake from the machine and shake out on to a wire rack to cool. Brush the warm, melted marmalade over the cake to glaze.

Spicy carrot cake

MAKES 10 SLICES

PER SLICE: 660 cals; 34g fat; 88g carbohydrate

225g (8oz) unsalted butter, softened

225g (8oz) light muscovado sugar

1 tbsp ground ginger

1 tsp ground cinnamon

250g (9oz) self-raising flour

2 tsp baking powder

50g (2oz) ground almonds

1 tsp almond extract

4 large eggs

300g (10oz) carrots, peeled and grated

100g (3½oz) sultanas

FOR THE ICING

200g (7oz) cream cheese

350g (12oz) golden icing sugar

2 tsp lemon juice

This is one of the best cakes to bake in the bread machine. The carrots and dried fruit keep the rich, spicy sponge moist, and impart a lovely flavour. A tangy cream cheese frosting is the perfect complement.

1 Grease and line the bread maker bucket with baking parchment, if specified in the manual.

2 Put the butter, sugar and ground spices in a large bowl and beat with an electric whisk until softened. Add the flour, baking powder, ground almonds, almond extract and eggs, and beat until combined. Add the carrots and sultanas and stir in gently.

3 Turn the mixture into the bread bucket and level the surface. Fit the bucket into the bread maker and set to the cake or bake only programme. Select 1¼ hours on the timer and choose a light crust. Press start.

4 To check whether the cake is done, pierce the centre with a skewer; it should come out fairly clean. If necessary re-set the timer for a little longer. Remove the bucket from the machine, leave the cake in it for 10 minutes, then transfer to a wire rack to cool.

5 To make the icing, beat the cream cheese in a bowl to soften. Sift the icing sugar into the bowl, add the lemon juice and beat well until smooth and creamy. Spread the icing over the top and sides of the cake, swirling it with a palette knife.

Chocolate fruit and nut cake

MAKES 10 SLICES

PER SLICE: 510 cals; 29g fat; 61g carbohydrate

200g (7oz) bar fruit and nut milk chocolate
175g (6oz) unsalted butter, softened
175g (6oz) golden caster sugar
3 large eggs
250g (9oz) self-raising flour
1 tsp baking powder
200g (7oz) chocolate and hazelnut spread
2 tbsp milk

A quick and easy cake that uses a large bar of fruit and nut chocolate to provide three ingredients in one. Chopped up and mixed into the sponge, the chocolate develops a slightly fudgy taste and lends a crunchy texture.

1 Grease and line the bread maker bucket with baking parchment, if specified in the manual. Chop the chocolate into 1cm (½in) pieces.

2 Put the butter, sugar, eggs, flour and baking powder into a bowl and beat with an electric whisk for 2 minutes until pale and creamy. Beat in half of the chocolate and hazelnut spread, together with the milk. Stir in half the chopped chocolate.

3 Turn the mixture into the bread bucket and level the surface. Scatter the remaining chopped chocolate over the surface, pressing it down gently into the mixture.

4 Fit the bucket into the bread maker and set to the cake or bake only programme. Select 1 hour 10 minutes on the timer and choose a light crust. Press start.

5 To check whether the cake is done, press the centre with your hand; it should feel firm. If necessary, set the timer for a little longer. Remove the bucket from the machine, leave the cake in it for 5 minutes, then transfer to a wire rack to cool.

6 Once cooled, spread the top of the cake with the remaining chocolate spread, swirling it attractively with a palette knife.

Coconut cream cake

MAKES 8 SLICES

PER SLICE: 440 cals; 28g fat; 45g carbohydrate

100g (3½oz) creamed coconut, chopped into small
    pieces
150g (5oz) unsalted butter, softened
175g (6oz) golden caster sugar
3 large eggs
1 tsp almond extract
finely grated zest of 1 lemon
225g (8oz) self-raising flour
1 tsp baking powder
2 tsp shredded or desiccated coconut to sprinkle
Icing sugar to dust

Creamed coconut gives this simple cake a smooth, creamy, rich flavour and reduces the risk of dryness that's sometimes encountered with the more familiar desiccated coconut. This isn't an overly sweet cake, and it's especially good served topped with good quality cherry preserve.

1 Grease and line the bread maker bucket with baking parchment, if specified in the manual. Put the creamed coconut pieces in a bowl and microwave on full powder for 1–2 minutes until softened.

2 Beat the butter, sugar and softened coconut together in a bowl using an electric whisk until creamy. Add the eggs, almond extract, lemon zest, flour and baking powder, and beat again until pale and creamy.

3 Turn the mixture into the bread maker bucket and level the surface. Sprinkle with the shredded coconut.

4 Fit the bucket into the bread maker and set to the cake or bake only programme. Select 45 minutes on the timer and choose a light crust. Press start.

5 To check whether the cake is done, pierce the centre with a skewer; it should come out fairly clean. If necessary re-set the timer for a little longer.

6 Remove the bucket from the machine and turn the cake out on to a wire rack to cool. Serve dusted with icing sugar.

Espresso and walnut cake

MAKES 10 SLICES

PER SLICE: 430 cals; 26g fat; 46g carbohydrate

100g (3½oz) walnuts, plus extra to sprinkle

1½ tbsp instant espresso coffee

1 tbsp boiling water

175g (6oz) unsalted butter, softened

175g (6oz) light muscovado sugar

3 large eggs, lightly beaten

225g (8oz) self-raising flour

½ tsp baking powder

FOR THE BUTTERCREAM

50g (2oz) unsalted butter, softened

100g (3½oz) golden icing sugar

1 tsp hot water

Chopped walnuts and espresso coffee give this cake a chunky texture and rich flavour. If you like a really strong coffee flavour, simply dissolve a bit more espresso coffee in the water.

1 Chop the walnuts fairly finely. Mix the coffee with the 1 tbsp boiling water and stir until dissolved. Grease and line the bread maker bucket with baking parchment, if specified in the manual.

2 Put the butter and sugar in a large bowl and beat well with an electric whisk until very pale and creamy. Gradually beat in the eggs a little at a time, beating well after each addition, and adding a little of the flour if the mixture starts to curdle. Stir in the coffee and chopped nuts.

3 Sift the flour and baking powder into the bowl and stir in. Turn the mixture into the bread bucket and level the surface.

4 Fit the bucket into the bread maker and set to the cake or bake only programme. Select 50 minutes on the timer and choose a light crust. Press start.

5 To check whether the cake is done, pierce the centre with a skewer; it should come out fairly clean. If necessary, re-set the timer for a little longer. Remove the bucket from the machine, leave the cake in it for 5 minutes, then transfer to a wire rack to cool.

6 To make the buttercream, put the butter and icing sugar in a bowl and beat well until smooth. Add 1 tsp hot water and beat until pale and creamy. Spread the buttercream over the top of the cake, roughly forking it decoratively. Scatter with extra chopped walnuts to finish.

Lavender and lemon cake

MAKES 8 SLICES

PER SLICE: 480 cals; 21g fat; 70g carbohydrate

8 large flowering lavender sprigs
175g (6oz) unsalted butter, softened
175g (6oz) golden caster sugar
3 large eggs
250g (9oz) self-raising flour
1 tsp baking powder
Finely grated zest of 1 lemon

FOR THE ICING

2 flowering lavender sprigs
175g (6oz) golden icing sugar
2 tbsp lemon juice

Lavender's long flowering season provides plenty of opportunities for you to make this deliciously fragrant Madeira style cake, with its tangy icing.

1 Grease and line the bread maker bucket with baking parchment, if specified in the manual. Pull the lavender flowers from their sprigs.

2 Put the butter, sugar, eggs, flour, baking powder, lemon zest and lavender flowers in a large mixing bowl and beat with an electric whisk for 2 minutes until pale and creamy. Turn the mixture into the bread bucket and level the surface.

3 Fit the bucket into the bread maker and set to the cake or bake only programme. Select 50 minutes on the timer and choose a light crust. Press start.

4 To check whether the cake is done, pierce the centre with a skewer; it should come out fairly clean. If necessary re-set the timer and cook a little longer.

5 Remove the bucket from the machine, leave the cake in it for 5 minutes, then transfer to a wire rack to cool.

6 Make the icing while the cake is still warm. Strip the lavender flowers from their sprigs and put them in a bowl. Sift the icing sugar into the bowl, add the lemon juice and beat thoroughly until smooth.

7 Spoon the icing on top of the warm cake and spread it to the edges. Leave to cool.

Index